"In harmony with the Bible and Christian tradition, Stephen Wellum has provided us with a robust defense of a high Christology, one 'from above,' which is desperately needed in our day of confusion and groundless speculation about the identity of Christ. This work shows us biblically and theologically why the church must affirm the full deity and full humanity of Christ. A five-star rating!"

Michael A. G. Haykin, Chair and Professor of Church History, The Southern Baptist Theological Seminary

"Jesus's pressing question to his disciples 'But who do you say that I am?' remains as urgent as ever. In contrast to modern historical critics who 'go low' in their quest for the historical Jesus, Stephen Wellum 'goes high,' engaging Christology 'from above' in order to identify Jesus as the Christ. He rightly views Jesus's person and work in the interpretive framework of the Bible's storyline and the tradition of historic orthodoxy to which the faithful reading of Scripture has given rise."

Kevin J. Vanhoozer, Research Professor of Systematic Theology, Trinity Evangelical Divinity School

"Stephen Wellum's study of the person of Christ is the first I recommend on the subject. His grasp of the historical, theological, and exegetical issues is firm, and his exposition is precise, clear, and contemporary—just what you want in a Christology."

Fred G. Zaspel, Executive Editor, Books at a Glance; Pastor, Reformed Baptist Church, Franconia, Pennsylvania

"Stephen Wellum distills years of reflection and scholarly writing on Christology into an easy-to-read form. In brief compass, he leads the reader through the biblical foundations for the doctrine of Christ's person and work and then through the historical debates in which the language of Christological orthodoxy was forged and refined. There is deep material here, but Wellum has a gift for expressing even the most subtle of theological issues with clarity and conciseness."

Carl R. Trueman, Professor of Biblical and Religious Studies, Grove City College

"To this day, there is no shortage of answers to Jesus's question 'Who do you say that I am?' That is why Stephen Wellum's *The Person of Christ* is sorely needed. Wellum offers the church a vital resource to help us regain a biblical and orthodox understanding of the person of Christ. If you want to grow and help others grow in the knowledge of ~~~~ his book."

Juan R. Sanchez, Sen ~~~~ h, Austin, Texas; author, *The L*

T0339033

"Clearly written, biblically driven, and historically grounded, this volume paints a theologically faithful portrait of Jesus. What could be more important for the church?"

Christopher W. Morgan, Dean, School of Christian Ministries and Professor of Theology, California Baptist University

"I require my seminary students to read Stephen Wellum's *God the Son Incarnate* because he masterfully answers seemingly contradictory claims about Jesus by integrating exegesis, biblical theology, historical theology, and systematic theology. This book is shorter, more accessible, and less intimidating—an ideal entry point for someone who wants to better understand who Christ is."

Andy Naselli, Associate Professor of Systematic Theology and New Testament, Bethlehem College & Seminary; Elder, Bethlehem Baptist Church

"Drawing on the biblical witness and on the insights of the greatest minds of the Christian centuries, this volume by Stephen Wellum, set firmly in the context of classical theism, provides a comprehensive answer to the most important of all questions: 'Who is Jesus Christ?' Clear but not cold, accessible but not shallow, this book will both inspire the novice and refresh the veteran."

Donald MacLeod, Professor Emeritus of Systematic Theology, Edinburgh Theological Seminary; author, *A Faith to Live By* and *The Person of Christ*

"Stephen Wellum is the first contemporary guide I would turn to for a scripturally faithful, confessionally orthodox Christology. This brief but meaty work not only feeds the mind but is a rich feast for the whole soul. You will worship Christ with fresh vigor at every turn of the page."

Scott Christensen, Associate Pastor, Kerrville Bible Church, Kerrville, Texas; author, *What about Free Will?* and *What about Evil?*

"Stephen Wellum has proved himself to be a trusted guide through the lurking dangers that scatter the theological landscape. This volume is concise and accessible, written for folks who desire to engage theological depth without being overwhelmed. It will serve well students who desire serious consideration of the second person of the Trinity, our Lord Jesus Christ."

Ardel B. Caneday, Retired Professor of New Testament Studies and Greek, University of Northwestern, St. Paul, Minnesota

"This book presents the basic biblical, historical, and systematic material essential to understanding the orthodox and biblical doctrine of Christ. It is an ideal first book to read on the central doctrine of the person of Christ for students and a great review for pastors and lay leaders."

Craig A. Carter, Professor of Theology, Tyndale University; author, *Contemplating God with the Great Tradition*

"This is a superb introduction to Christology. Stephen Wellum helps readers think about the very nature of theology itself at the most profound level, explicated for the reader with Christology as a test case in how to do theology. And the reader is given a rich treatment of how to think about Christology in terms of the biblical-theological substructure of the Bible itself and how to wrestle with contemporary challenges. Excellent."

Bradley G. Green, Professor of Theological Studies, Union University

"There is nothing more important than getting the right response to the question 'Who do you say that Jesus is?' In *The Person of Christ*, Stephen Wellum answers the question by grounding the response in the Scriptures, by guiding readers through historical theology, and by summarizing these teachings and truths theologically. As a tour de force on the person of Christ and the doctrine of Christology, this work also serves as a model for how one moves from the Bible to theology to life."

Gregory C. Strand, Executive Director of Theology and Credentialing, Evangelical Free Church of America; Adjunct Professor of Pastoral Theology, Trinity Evangelical Divinity School

"Stephen Wellum is a theologian who loves the church, and in *The Person of Christ*, he brings his seasoned expertise on Christology to equip thinking Christians with a concise introduction to the subject. In three accessible sections, he provides a biblical foundation for who Christ is, surveys how the church came to understand and express Christological orthodoxy, and explains why churches need to keep Christ at the center of their life and gospel ministry. If you are looking to understand Christology more clearly and worship Christ more deeply, this is your book."

David S. Schrock, Pastor of Preaching and Theology, Occoquan Bible Church; Professor of Theology, Indianapolis Theological Seminary

SHORT STUDIES IN SYSTEMATIC THEOLOGY

Edited by Graham A. Cole and Oren R. Martin

The Person of Christ

An Introduction

Stephen J. Wellum

CROSSWAY®

WHEATON, ILLINOIS

Library of Congress Cataloging-in-Publication Data

Names: Wellum, Stephen J., 1964– author.
Title: The person of Christ : an introduction / Stephen J. Wellum.
Description: Wheaton, Illinois : Crossway, 2021. | Series: Short studies in systematic theology | Includes bibliographical references and index.
Identifiers: LCCN 2020013763 (print) | LCCN 2020013764 (ebook) | ISBN 9781433569432 (trade paperback) | ISBN 9781433569449 (pdf) | ISBN 9781433569456 (mobi) | ISBN 9781433569463 (epub)
Subjects: LCSH: Jesus Christ—Person and offices.
Classification: LCC BT203 .W4545 2021 (print) | LCC BT203 (ebook) | DDC 232/.8—dc23
LC record available at https://lccn.loc.gov/2020013763
LC ebook record available at https://lccn.loc.gov/2020013764

VP   30   29   28   27   26   25   24   23   22   21
15   14   13   12   11   10   9   8   7   6   5   4   3   2   1

To my in-laws, Charles and Margaret Hackenberry:

Thankful for your faithfulness in marriage and as parents,
and grateful for your example to know, love,
and proclaim Christ Jesus as Lord.

Contents

PART 3
THEOLOGICAL SUMMARY
The Orthodox Identity of Our Lord Jesus Christ

Series Preface

The ancient Greek thinker Heraclitus reputedly said that the thinker has to listen to the essence of things. A series of theological studies dealing with the traditional topics that make up systematic theology needs to do just that. Accordingly, in each of these studies, a theologian addresses the essence of a doctrine. This series thus aims to present short studies in theology that are attuned to both the Christian tradition and contemporary theology in order to equip the church to faithfully understand, love, teach, and apply what God has revealed in Scripture about a variety of topics. What may be lost in comprehensiveness can be gained through what John Calvin, in the dedicatory epistle of his commentary on Romans, called "lucid brevity."

Of course, a thorough study of any doctrine will be longer rather than shorter, as there are two millennia of confession, discussion, and debate with which to interact. As a result, a short study needs to be more selective but deftly so. Thankfully, the contributors to this series have the ability to be brief yet accurate. The key aim is that the simpler is not to morph into the simplistic. The test is whether the topic of a short study, when further studied in depth, requires some unlearning to take place. The simple can be amplified. The simplistic needs to be corrected. As editors, we believe that the volumes in this series pass that test.

While the specific focus varies, each volume (1) introduces the doctrine, (2) sets it in context, (3) develops it from Scripture, (4) draws the various threads together, and (5) brings it to bear on the Christian life. It is our prayer, then, that this series will assist the church to delight in her triune God by thinking his thoughts—which he has graciously revealed in his written word, which testifies to his living Word, Jesus Christ—after him in the powerful working of his Spirit.

Graham A. Cole and Oren R. Martin

Introduction

Who Do You Say That Jesus Is?

The question Jesus asked his disciples many years ago is still alive and well today: "Who do people say that I am?" (Mark 8:27). As in the first century, so today there is much confusion regarding Jesus's identity, even though from a merely historical perspective, Jesus is the most towering figure in all history.[1] The disciples responded to Jesus's question by listing some of the diverse answers of their day: "Some say John the Baptist; others say Elijah; and still others, one of the prophets" (Mark 8:28 NIV). What all these answers have in common is the acknowledgment that Jesus is extraordinary, but they all keep him in the category of a mere human.

Today, similar to the first century, people continue to answer Jesus's question with diverse and confused answers. For some, Jesus is viewed as a great prophet or a wise philosopher, an important religious leader or even a social-justice revolutionary who took on the establishment. But again, what current views

---

1. See Jaroslav Pelikan, *Jesus through the Centuries: His Place in the History of Culture* (New Haven, CT: Yale University Press, 1999), 1. Pelikan writes, "Regardless of what anyone may personally think or believe about him, Jesus of Nazareth has been the dominant figure in the history of Western culture for almost twenty centuries."

have in common with the older answers is that Jesus is merely a noteworthy man. So as various polls demonstrate, people have diverse views about Jesus but views that are confused, often contradictory, and, sadly, not what Scripture says about him.[2]

In stark contrast to the diverse views of Jesus in the first century and today, Scripture, along with the creeds of the church, presents a consistent, clear answer to Jesus's question. Jesus *is* the divine Son, the second person of the triune Godhead, the Lord of glory, who in time assumed a human nature, so that now and forevermore he is the eternal "Word made flesh" (cf. John 1:1, 14). And he did this because it's only one individual—God the Son incarnate—who can bring about God's eternal plan by securing our redemption, executing judgment on sin, and establishing a new creation by the ratification of a new covenant in his life, death, and resurrection.

For this reason, the Jesus of the Bible who is the true Jesus is unique, exclusive, and the only Lord and Savior: "There is salvation in no one else, for there is no other name under heaven given among men by which we must be saved" (Acts 4:12). This is also why confusion about him is a matter of life and death. Nothing is more important than getting right *who* Jesus is. The question of Jesus's identity is not merely academic, something for theologians to ponder; it's a question vital for all people to consider—and *especially* for the contemporary evangelical church.

We live in a day when people are greatly confused about Jesus's identity. We are surrounded by a growing rejection of Christian theology, a rising militant secularism, and a rampant philosophical and religious pluralism. All this has contributed to people's confusion regarding who Jesus is. But sadly, this confu-

---

2. George Gallup Jr. and George O'Connell, *Who Do Americans Say That I Am?* (Philadelphia: Westminster, 1986).

sion is not merely outside the evangelical church; it's also within. In 2018, Ligonier Ministries and LifeWay Research conducted a poll among self-identified evangelicals and issued the results in their *State of Theology* report.[3] Reflected in many of the answers is evidence that our churches suffer a serious lack of biblical and theological knowledge, especially regarding *who* Jesus is. Two questions are especially alarming. When given the statement "Jesus is the first and greatest being created by God," 78 percent agreed. Yet anyone with a rudimentary knowledge of Scripture and Christological orthodoxy should have recognized that this is a denial of Christ's deity and an embrace of the ancient heresy of Arianism (or the current view of Jehovah's Witnesses). Not surprisingly, when given the statement "God accepts the worship of all religions, including Christianity, Judaism, and Islam," 51 percent agreed. If Jesus's identity is misunderstood, inevitably Jesus's exclusive work will also be compromised.

No doubt, polls are often tricky to judge, but regardless, it does reveal a serious need for the ongoing careful teaching and exposition of *who* Jesus is from Scripture and the church's confessional standards. Repeatedly, Scripture exhorts the church in every generation to faithfully "preach the word" and to "reprove, rebuke, and exhort, with complete patience and teaching" (2 Tim. 4:2). Our goal in doing so is to see the church built up "until we all attain to the unity of the faith and of the knowledge of the Son of God" (Eph. 4:13). We do not want the church to be "tossed to and fro by the waves and carried about by every wind of doctrine" (Eph. 4:14), especially in regard to *who* Jesus is!

For this reason, a study in Christology that seeks to explain *who* Jesus is from Scripture and historical theology, *why* Jesus is unique, and *how* we are to think theologically about the

---

3. *The State of Theology*, Ligonier, accessed May 7, 2020, https://thestateoftheology.com/.

incarnation is always necessary but is especially urgent today given the serious confusion that exists both outside and within the church. Despite this book being only a "short study" in Christology, my goal is to equip the church to know the basic biblical teaching about who Jesus is *and* how the church has theologically confessed the identity of Jesus throughout the ages.[4] If a longer treatment of the person of Christ is required, the reader is encouraged to consult my larger work on the same subject: *God the Son Incarnate: The Doctrine of Christ* (Crossway, 2016). In that work, I place the study of who Jesus is within various debates of Western intellectual history and at every point give a more detailed exposition and defense of orthodox Christology. This shorter work, however, is designed to be more accessible to the average reader and thus is ideal for pastors, church leaders, and Christians who want to know what Scripture says about our Lord Jesus and how the church has consistently proclaimed Christ Jesus as Lord. Although some of the material in this volume is adapted from my book *God the Son Incarnate*, owing to parallel arguments and a similar arrangement of topics and material, it's not a mere abridgment of the earlier work. This work not only thoroughly develops the previous material but also expands on a number of points that the previous work only hinted at, especially regarding the relations of persons within the Trinity and the work of the Holy Spirit in the life of the incarnate Son.[5]

To accomplish the goal of equipping the church to know the basic biblical teaching about who Jesus is and the confessional tradition of the church, the book is written in three parts.

---

4. For a longer treatment of each of the areas covered in this shorter work, see Stephen J. Wellum, *God the Son Incarnate: The Doctrine of Christ*, Foundations of Evangelical Theology (Wheaton, IL: Crossway, 2016).

5. Any material adapted from *God the Son Incarnate* in this work is used by permission of Crossway.

Part 1 lays out the basic biblical data regarding Jesus's identity as presented across the Bible's storyline, after briefly discussing some important methodological points on how to construct a biblically faithful, theologically orthodox Christology. Part 2 turns to historical theology and thinks through how the church faithfully "put together" the biblical data and made theological judgments about Christ consistent with Scripture. In light of various false ways of thinking about who Jesus is—heresies still with us today—the church confessed Jesus's identity in faithfulness to Scripture and with theological precision, a confession and orthodoxy we need to follow today. Part 3 offers a systematic theological summary of who Jesus is as God the Son incarnate from Scripture and in light of the confessional orthodoxy of the church. In a summary way, it attempts to answer questions often asked about Christ's identity and the nature of the incarnation.

Ultimately, my goal in writing this book is to help the church know the Lord Jesus according to Scripture and thus in all his glory and majesty, to lead the church to trust him more as our only Lord and Savior, and to equip the church to articulate a Christological orthodoxy in continuity with the "faith that was once for all delivered to the saints" (Jude 3).

PART 1

Biblical Foundations

Understanding the Identity of Christ

1

Approaching Scripture on Its Own Terms to Identify Christ

Throughout the ages, the church has consistently confessed that Jesus of Nazareth is God the Son incarnate and thus the only Lord and Savior. On what epistemological grounds has the church made this confession? On the basis of God's authoritative word-revelation that alone warrants such a theological confession about Jesus. Thus, to know *who* Jesus is and to speak rightly of him, the church, from its first days, has done Christology *from above*, namely, from the vantage point of Scripture. The Bible—first the Old Testament and then the New—has provided not only the "facts" about Jesus but also the interpretive framework for understanding Jesus's identity. The church knows that she can correctly identify *who* Jesus is only by placing him in the context of the Bible's storyline, teaching, and worldview. In fact, any attempt to do Christology by some other means leads only to a Jesus of our own imagination.

Since the rise of the Enlightenment, starting in the seventeenth century, however, these theological and methodological convictions were gradually viewed as no longer credible. During this era, Christology was done on other theological grounds that resulted in a Jesus who is a masterful religious leader but not the Word made flesh. Why did this occur? Although the answer is complex, it was primarily due to entire worldview shifts. Over the last four hundred years, we have witnessed the truth of the old adage "Ideas have consequences." After the Reformation era, certain "ideas" arose that challenged and then rejected the way the church, and most people in the West, thought about God and his relationship to the world. More specifically, ideas about the power of human reason, the nature of reality, and our knowledge of that reality led to crucial shifts in "plausibility structures." Beginning with the Enlightenment and continuing through modernism and now postmodernism, the intellectual rules that determine how people think the world works and what is possible have shifted away from historic Christianity to deny its basic theological convictions. This is why many in the West stumble over the church's confession of who Jesus is. For many, it does not seem plausible or rationally coherent.[1]

In his magisterial work on the impact of secularization on our thinking, Charles Taylor traces these epistemological changes over three distinct time periods, pivoting around the Enlightenment. By doing so, he explains why our age finds it implausible to begin with the basic truths of Christian theology and why the rules that warrant belief have changed. Before the Enlightenment, people found it *impossible not to believe* the Christian worldview; starting with the Enlightenment, it became *possible not to believe* in the basic truths of Christian-

---

1. See Colin Brown, *Jesus in European Protestant Thought, 1778–1860* (Grand Rapids, MI: Baker, 1985).

ity; three hundred years after the Enlightenment, most people find it *impossible to believe* in the objective truths of Christian theology.[2] David Wells makes the same point. He contends that today theology is done within a twofold reality: first, "the disintegration of the Enlightenment world and its replacement by the postmodern ethos" and, second, the increase of religious pluralism.[3]

What impact have these changes had on Christology? Many, but most significantly, they have led to people thinking that the church's confession of Christ is implausible. People assume either that the Bible's Jesus could not exist or that he could not do what the Bible says he did. As such, people have questioned the church's confession of Christ's uniqueness and exclusivity as God the Son incarnate. Gotthold Lessing's question asked many years ago is alive and well: "How can one man who lived and died years ago have *universal* significance for all people?" Today, most people think of Jesus as one religious leader among many—a belief, sadly, that seems to have infiltrated the evangelical church.[4]

How should we respond? A full response would require a defense of the entire Christian worldview, which is not the purpose of this book. Instead, my focus is on the theological method undergirding such a defense, especially in relation to doing Christology. My argument is this: consistent with what the church has done in the past, what is needed is *not* a Christology *from below* but one that is *from above*. Before I explain why this is so, let me first define how I am using the terms *from below* and *from above*.

---

2. See Charles Taylor, *A Secular Age* (Cambridge, MA: Belknap Press of Harvard University Press, 2007).

3. David F. Wells, *Above All Earthly Pow'rs: Christ in a Postmodern World* (Grand Rapids, MI: Eerdmans, 2005), 5.

4. See statement nos. 3 and 6 of *The State of Theology*, Ligonier, accessed May 7, 2020, https://thestateoftheology.com/.

Christology from Below versus from Above

The phrases *from below* and *from above* are sometimes defined in different ways. By *from below*, I mean the attempt to do Christology from the vantage point of historical-critical research, independent of a commitment to the full authority of Scripture and a Christian-theistic worldview. Such an approach is critical of Scripture and assumes that the "Jesus of history" is *not* the "Jesus of the Bible." Conversely, a Christology *from above* starts with the triune God of Scripture and *his* word, and it seeks to identify Jesus's person and work from within the truth of Scripture.

Every interpretation and formulation of Christ's identity depends on and derives from a presuppositional nexus of philosophical and theological commitments. Any attempt to say *who* Jesus is and define his significance for the world assumes entire viewpoints regarding who and what God is, humanity is, and so on, and how we warrant these beliefs. From the beginning, the church has argued that to do Christology properly, we must do so under Scripture. To know Christ, we must do so from a revelational epistemology and the truth of the biblical worldview.

On the other hand, a Christology from below attempts to reconstruct the historical Jesus by critical methods to determine what we can know from Scripture. The problems with such an approach are manifold. Its central problem, however, is that before one can theologize about Christ, the critic must first establish what is and is not accurate in the Bible's presentation of him, which too often is governed by non-Christian theological and philosophical assumptions, specifically some form of methodological naturalism. It's not surprising that the Jesus from below is not the Jesus of the Bible but often a reflection of the person doing the investigation. For this reason, the church has argued that what is needed is a Christology from above.

Why Christology Must Be from Above

First, Christology must be from above because if Scripture is not the necessary and sufficient condition to warrant our Christological conclusions, then ultimately we will not be able to say anything objectively true and theological about Christ's identity. A Christology from below must first decide which historical facts about Jesus in Scripture are true and, more importantly, when (if ever) the biblical author's theological interpretation of Jesus is accurate. If the historical Jesus is not identical to the biblical Jesus, then critics must establish criteria outside Scripture to warrant what is true and theological about Christ. But what exactly are those criteria? Human rationality? Religious experience? The "assured" results of biblical scholarship? And who decides on the criteria? This kind of approach assumes from the outset that the triune God has not spoken authoritatively to us.

Since the Enlightenment, this approach has been tried by various "quests for the historical Jesus"—quests that still affect us today.[5] The goal of the quests was to recover the "Jesus of history," who is not identical to the "Jesus of the Bible," by peeling back the biblical layers of legend and myth via the historical-critical method. It's crucial to note that the starting point and conclusion of the quests mark a sharp turn away from orthodox Christology, as they operate on worldview assumptions foreign to Scripture.

The old, or first, quest (1778–1906)[6] refused to interpret the biblical text in terms of its own claims, content, and interpretive

---

5. On the quests, see Brown, *Jesus in European Protestant Thought*; N. T. Wright, *Jesus and the Victory of God*, vol. 2 in *Christian Origins and the Question of God* (Minneapolis: Fortress, 1997), 1–124; Alister E. McGrath, *The Making of Modern German Christology, 1750–1990*, 2nd ed. (Eugene, OR: Wipf and Stock, 2005).

6. As the first, the old quest received its name from the English title of Albert Schweitzer's book *The Quest of the Historical Jesus: A Critical Study of Its Progress from Reimarus to Wrede*, trans. William Montgomery (New York: Macmillan, 1968).

framework. These theologians assumed that the Bible is wholly unreliable and proceeded to reconstruct the "historical" Jesus without reliance on and almost without reference to the biblical presentation. The first half of the twentieth century brought an interim period (1906–1953)—called the "no quest"[7]—in which some theologians determined that historical facts were not necessary for the Christian faith. The difficulty of establishing any historical knowledge consistent with Enlightenment epistemologies and the tools of the historical-critical method shifted the problem momentarily from the Bible's historicity to its mythology. For example, Rudolf Bultmann simply replaced the New Testament's so-called mythological framework with an existential framework, but he rejected the Bible's own theological framework and worldview understanding.[8]

The new, or second, quest (1953 to present) focuses on the *kerygma* ("proclamation") about Jesus in Scripture, being dissatisfied with the doubts of the old quest and the radical skepticism of the no quest.[9] These theologians agree with the other quests that the Gospel traditions are interpretations of the early church, but they believe that the Gospels contain true historical facts, which they seek to recover. Yet the new quest remains firmly committed to methodological naturalism, and the rules they employ to discover the historical Jesus are independent of historic Christian theology.[10]

---

7. W. Barnes Tatum, *In Quest of Jesus: A Guidebook* (Atlanta: John Knox, 1982), 71.

8. Rudolf Bultmann, *New Testament and Mythology and Other Basic Writings*, ed. and trans. Schubert M. Ogden (Philadelphia: Fortress, 1984), 5–6.

9. For example, see Ernst Käsemann, "The Problem of the Historical Jesus," in *Essays on New Testament Themes*, trans. W. J. Montague (1964; repr., London: SCM, 2012), 15–47; James M. Robinson, *A New Quest of the Historical Jesus and Other Essays* (Minneapolis: Fortress, 1983).

10. *Methodological naturalism* is the view that for any study of the world to be legitimate, including the study of history and theology, all cause-effect relationships must be explained naturalistically and without reference to God's unique and extraordinary action in the world. As such, this view rejects the possibility of God's miraculous action in the world from the outset.

At the same time, the third quest (early 1980s to present)[11] follows its own modified version of historical-critical criteria. In general, it applies the rules for authenticity more generously in an attempt to take the New Testament texts seriously as literary documents with basic (but not full) reliability. These theologians also take seriously the Jewish context of early Christianity—a context often disregarded by the other quests. But for many in this movement, these conciliatory efforts are still not a return to the full authority of Scripture, which results in the problem of not saying anything theological and universally significant about Jesus.

Ultimately, each quest struggles to establish criteria and warrant. If Scripture is unreliable because it's a mixture of fact and fiction, then it alone cannot serve as the theological warrant for our Christology. The authority and reliability of Scripture is the precondition for the possibility of doing Christology in an objective, normative way. Without divine speech that reveals both the true facts about Jesus and the authoritative interpretation of his identity, Christology loses its truthfulness, and Christ's uniqueness is set adrift in the sea of pluralism. As Francis Watson correctly observes, "Historical research is unlikely to confirm an incarnation or a risen Lord."[12] And even if a reconstructed Jesus is a figure of some significance, "he cannot be identified with the Christ of faith acknowledged by the church."[13] The heirs of the Enlightenment only exacerbate the problem of reconstructing the past by assuming that historical events are self-interpreting and transparent to historical

---

11. On the third quest, see Ben Witherington, III, *The Jesus Quest: The Third Search for the Jew of Nazareth*, 2nd ed. (Downers Grove, IL: InterVarsity Press, 1997).

12. Francis Watson, "*Veritas Christi*: How to Get from the Jesus of History to the Christ of Faith without Losing One's Way," in *Seeking the Identity of Jesus: A Pilgrimage*, ed. Beverly Roberts Gaventa and Richard B. Hays (Grand Rapids, MI: Eerdmans, 2008), 104.

13. Watson, "*Veritas Christi*," 105.

investigation. Historical research alone can never yield an objective and infallibly true interpretation of Jesus's identity and significance.

Correctly identifying Jesus, then, requires God himself to disclose the historical facts *and* the theological significance of those facts. A Christology from below undercuts the epistemological grounds for orthodoxy and leaves a normative Christology problematic. Only a Christology from above provides the warrant for the Bible's and the church's *theological* confession of Christ.

Second, a Christology from below fails to ground the uniqueness and universal significance of Jesus because it removes him from the Bible's storyline and interpretive framework. Orthodox Christology requires a specific soil in which to grow, and a Christology from below removes Jesus from the life-giving soil of Scripture. We can grasp Jesus's uniqueness and universal significance only by leaving him firmly planted in the triune God's eternal plan given in Scripture. If Jesus is removed from it, he will lose his true identity as the divine Son who has become human for us and our salvation (John 1:1–18); he will become an enigma to us, susceptible to various imaginative and arbitrary constructions. This is the problem for those who think that historical facts about Jesus, specifically his bodily resurrection, carry their own meaning apart from placing Jesus and his resurrection within the overall plan of God given by Scripture.

For example, Wolfhart Pannenberg represents a Christology from below with all its attendant problems.[14] Pannenberg first argues that historical facts, discerned by historical research, carry their own meaning and thus allow us to say something

---

14. See Wolfhart Pannenberg, *Jesus: God and Man*, trans. Lewis L. Wilkins and Duane A. Priebe, 2nd ed. (Philadelphia: Westminster, 1977); Pannenberg, *Systematic Theology*, trans. Geoffrey W. Bromiley, 3 vols. (Grand Rapids, MI: Eerdmans, 1992), 1:277–396.

theological about Christ. He fudges slightly, however, because he also knows that to say something truly theological (universal, objectively true), Christ's resurrection must be placed within the "apocalyptic framework" of later Judaism.[15] Why? Apart from placing Christ's resurrection in this "universal" framework, we could not conclude that Jesus is unique and thus say anything theological about him. Thus, for Pannenberg, historical research, set in a specific "universal" framework, allows us to do Christology from below.

Pannenberg is correct on one point. To say anything theological about Jesus, we must place him within a universal interpretive grid. Pannenberg, however, faces a serious problem: the universal framework he depends on comes from Scripture, but for him, Scripture is not fully authoritative and true. How, then, can he appeal to Scripture if at many points it is inaccurate? What if the apocalyptic framework he uses is simply the mythological construction of Judaism and the early church? If so, then it carries no authority for Christology.

Colin Gunton asks these very questions of Pannenberg. Even if we grant, Gunton contends, that Pannenberg's Christology affirms the divine significance of Jesus, it's difficult to see how he has done so in a manner consistent with his method. As Gunton argues, to place historical facts within the Bible's interpretive framework without warranting it entails that he is "*either* presupposing some dogmatic beliefs ('context of meaning') and thus not arguing genuinely from below at all; *or* failing to establish what is wanted, namely, the divinity of Jesus."[16] Furthermore, Gunton charges Pannenberg with confusing two separate questions: "The first is that about the significance of Jesus within the context of interpretation—what

---

15. Pannenberg, *Jesus: God and Man*, 98.
16. Colin E. Gunton, *Yesterday and Today: A Study of Continuities in Christology*, 2nd ed. (London: SPCK, 1997), 21.

he meant to his contemporaries. The second is that concerning his significance now."[17] What has to be warranted, Gunton insists, is the acceptance of the Bible's framework of meaning for us today, but given Pannenberg's rejection of Scripture's full authority, how can he do so?

In truth, the only way we can warrant the theological claim that Jesus is the divine Son and that his incarnation and work have universal significance is by placing Christ's entire person and work within the plan of the triune God as given in Scripture when it is viewed as authoritative. Only a Christology from above will result in the *theological* Jesus of the Bible.

Orthodox Christology is rooted in a specific conception of God, Scripture, humans, and so on, and apart from that world-view, it cannot stand. To do Christology faithfully today, we must articulate and defend the theological system on which it stands. We must defend Trinitarian theism and Scripture as more than basically reliable. Orthodox Christology depends on specific truths for its coherence—truths that are warranted by the Bible alone. Scripture gives us a true account of history and a God's-eye viewpoint. Scripture is the word of the triune God speaking in and through human authors (2 Tim. 3:15–17; 2 Pet. 1:21), and as such, Scripture gives us God's own interpretation of his plan, centered on Christ. Apart from grounding who Jesus is in Scripture, orthodox Christology is not only implausible but impossible.

Third, a Christology from below cannot sustain Christian faith. As David Wells astutely observes, "Christologies constructed from 'below' produce only a larger-than-life religious figure, the perfection of what many others already experience."[18] Doing Christology from below never leads us

---

17. Gunton, *Yesterday and Today*, 21.

18. David F. Wells, *The Person of Christ: A Biblical and Historical Analysis of the Incarnation* (Westchester, IL: Crossway, 1984), 172.

to faith in God the Son, who came from above for us and our salvation. It's simply not possible to construct a biblical and orthodox Christology out of the fabric of human experience by historical-critical reconstruction. He will never be worthy of our worship.

For these reasons, it's necessary to do Christology from above. In doing so, we also stand in continuity with the church. The church has always done Christology from above. In fact, it's only a Christology from above that helps us see why we need Jesus as our only Lord and Savior. When we read Scripture, we discover how serious our sin is before God and why it's only God the Son incarnate who can save us. To stand justified before God, we need *this* Jesus alone in his representative and substitutionary work for us. Far from such an approach depreciating Jesus's humanity, it enhances it, because we learn that the kind of Savior we need must be fully God *and* fully human, Christ Jesus our Lord.

Doing Christology from Above and the Use of Scripture

The triune God and his word give us the epistemological warrant and worldview necessary to identify Jesus as God the Son incarnate and thus to speak theologically about him. A biblical Christology, then, must formulate Jesus's identity and the nature of the incarnation by carefully attending to the Bible's canonical presentation of him.

This task requires an intratextual approach to Scripture, namely, reading Scripture according to its own claims and presentation following the Bible's own categories and structure. For us to understand Jesus correctly, he must be placed within the Bible's own interpretive framework and authoritative teaching and not removed from it. Paul is a good illustration of this approach. When Paul goes to Athens (Acts 17:16–32), given that the Athenians are ignorant of even the most rudimentary truths that he needs to communicate, Paul preaches Christ by first sketching the biblical worldview, so as to make rational sense of who Christ is on the Bible's own terms. By starting with the God of creation, who humans are, and the nature of our problem, Paul sets the stage to proclaim Christ. Paul, then, makes *theological* sense of Jesus and demonstrates why he alone is Lord and Savior by placing him within the framework and categories of the Christian worldview.[19]

Furthermore, an intratextual approach assumes certain truths about Scripture: Scripture is God's word written through the free agency of human authors. As *God's* word, it gives us an authoritative interpretation of who Jesus is. Although Scripture is not exhaustive, even about Jesus (John 21:25), whatever it says, it says accurately and infallibly. There is, therefore, no distinction between the "Jesus of history" and the "Christ of faith"—a distinction that assumes that the Scriptures are unreliable in recounting and interpreting historical events.

In fact, recognizing that Scripture is given by God is the precondition for a normative Christology. Scripture alone serves as our norm for grasping Christ's identity. Removing Jesus from the Bible's storyline or accepting some parts and not others only leads to a subjective, arbitrary, and ultimately false construction of Jesus's identity. If we do not "interpret the biblical texts 'on their own terms,'"[20] making theological judgments according to Scripture's own teaching, then the Jesus constructed will not be the Jesus of the Bible. To read Scripture "on its own terms" entails that we read the entire canon and take seriously what it

---

19. On this point, see D. A. Carson, "Athens Revisited," in *Telling the Truth: Evangelizing Postmoderns*, ed. D. A. Carson (Grand Rapids, MI: Zondervan, 2000), 384–98.

20. Kevin J. Vanhoozer, "Exegesis and Hermeneutics," in *New Dictionary of Biblical Theology*, ed. T. Desmond Alexander and Brian S. Rosner (Downers Grove, IL: InterVarsity Press, 2000), 52.

says about God's mighty acts and how it interprets them, especially in regard to Christ. This means that Scripture describes the facts of history with accuracy and explains those facts so we can rightly know Christ and formulate correct doctrine about him. In doing Christology, then, we move carefully from Scripture's own teaching (first order) to theological formulation (second order).[21]

As we move from Scripture (canon) to theological formulation (concept), we must also take seriously the aid of tradition and historical theology. This is especially true in Christology. The confessions of Nicaea (325) and Chalcedon (451) are catholic, or universal, *rules of faith* in the church that define Christological orthodoxy, and we depart from them at our peril. They do not have this status because they are equal to Scripture but because they "put together" all the scriptural teaching in a faithful and coherent way. Systematic theology is more than simply repeating Scripture; it's the full practice of "faith seeking understanding," as Anselm famously put it. In fact, fully attending to Scripture drives us to make sense of it. For example, how do we make sense of Jesus as the Son in relation to the Father (John 5:16–30)? How do we make sense of the relationship between the Son's deity and humanity (John 1:1, 14)? How do we make sense of the fact that Jesus as God the Son knows all things yet also says that he does not know all things (Mark 13:32)? Questions like these legitimately arise from Scripture, and if we are faithful to Scripture, they require constructive theological reflection, which is precisely what doing Christology entails.

We must also remain clear, however, that historical theology and confessions as rules of faith are always subservient

---

21. See Richard Lints, *The Fabric of Theology: A Prolegomenon to Evangelical Theology* (Grand Rapids, MI: Eerdmans, 1993), 259–336.

to Scripture. Scripture as *norma normans* ("ruling rule") has magisterial authority over tradition. Tradition as *norma normata* ("ruled rule") functions in a ministerial capacity to aid our interpretation and application of Scripture. Stating the relationship between Scripture and tradition this way does not deny that reading Scripture involves a "hermeneutical spiral."[22] No one approaches Scripture as a tabula rasa (or "clean slate," without preconceived ideas); we all interpret Scripture with viewpoints, assumptions, and even biases. But Scripture is able to confirm or correct our views as needed precisely because Scripture is God's word written and is authoritative, clear, and sufficient for the doing of theology.

In the next three chapters, we turn to the biblical foundations for understanding Jesus's identity, before thinking through the church's confession of Jesus as the divine Son made flesh.

---

22. See, for example, Grant R. Osborne, *The Hermeneutical Spiral: A Comprehensive Introduction to Biblical Interpretation*, 2nd ed. (Downers Grove, IL: IVP Academic, 2010).

2

The Identity of Christ
from the Bible's Storyline

Who is Jesus? To answer this question, we must turn to Scripture, but first to the Old Testament. Why? Our understanding of who Jesus is and why he has come is given to us from the Bible's entire storyline, beginning in Genesis. Jesus does not come to us in a vacuum or *de novo*. Instead, the Jesus of the Bible comes to us from the entire Bible. Individual texts in the New Testament make sense only when they are placed in the context of the Old. To establish the *biblical* identity of Christ, we must do so from the entirety of Scripture.

In fact, as we trace the Bible's storyline—starting in creation, accounting for the fall, and unfolding God's promise of a coming Redeemer through the biblical covenants—we discover that the Bible unveils the teaching that Jesus is God the Son incarnate. In chapters 3–4, we turn to the New Testament data regarding Christ, but in this chapter, we sketch four truths, or building blocks, grounded in the Bible's covenantal storyline, that are necessary to set the stage for the New

Testament data and to make sense of who Jesus is and why he alone is Lord and Savior.

God as the Triune Creator–Covenant Lord[1]

Starting with God's identity to identify Christ might seem strange, but it's not. We cannot know who Jesus is, especially as the divine Son, apart from starting with the God of the Bible.

In fact, as noted in the previous chapter, this is where Paul begins at Athens (Acts 17:16–32). Given that the Athenians were steeped in idolatry, pluralistic in their outlook, and ignorant of the biblical worldview, Paul first builds a biblical-theological framework so that his proclamation of Jesus will make sense on the Bible's own terms. It's only *after* he has done this that he identifies who Jesus is from *within* the biblical worldview in order to establish his uniqueness and exclusivity as Lord and Savior. Even within the condensed address recorded in Acts 17, Paul begins his presentation with the doctrine of God and creation and then moves through redemptive history to the coming of Christ. By so doing, Paul explains who Jesus is within the frame and categories of Scripture. Indeed, as D. A. Carson reminds us, "The good news of Jesus Christ—who he is and what he accomplished by his death, resurrection, and exaltation—is simply incoherent unless certain structures are already in place. . . . One cannot make sense of the Bible's portrayal of Jesus without such blocks in place."[2] With that in mind, let's begin to identify who Jesus is by first identifying who God is.

---

1. This section is adapted from Stephen J. Wellum, "*Solus Christus*: What the Reformers Taught and Why It Still Matters," *Southern Baptist Journal of Theology* 19, no. 4 (2015): 79–107. Used by permission of *The Southern Baptist Journal of Theology*.

2. D. A. Carson, "Athens Revisited," in *Telling the Truth: Evangelizing Postmoderns*, ed. D. A. Carson (Grand Rapids, MI: Zondervan, 2000), 386.

God is the triune Creator–covenant Lord.[3] From the opening verses of Scripture, God is presented as the uncreated, independent, self-sufficient Creator of the universe who creates and rules all things by his word (Gen. 1–2; Ps. 50:12–14; Acts 17:24–25; cf. John 1:1). This truth establishes the central distinction of all theology: the Creator-creature distinction, which eliminates any pantheistic or panentheistic views of the God-world relationship. God alone is God; all else is creation and depends totally on him for life and everything. God's transcendent lordship (1 Kings 8:27; Pss. 7:17; 9:2; 21:7; 97:9; Isa. 6:1; Rev. 4:3) also eliminates any notion of deism, which rejects God's agency in human history; God is transcendent *and* immanent with his creation. As Creator, God is the covenant Lord who is fully present and related to his creatures: he freely, sovereignly, and purposefully sustains and governs all things to his desired end (Ps. 139:1–10; Acts 17:28; Eph. 1:11; 4:6), but he is not part of his world or developing with it.

As Creator and covenant Lord, God sovereignly and personally rules over his creation. He rules with perfect power, knowledge, and righteousness (Pss. 9:8; 33:5; 139:1–4, 16; Isa. 46:9–11; Acts 4:27–28; Rom. 11:33–36) as the only being who is independent and self-sufficient. As Lord, God acts in, with, and through his creatures to accomplish his plan and purposes (Eph. 1:11). As personal, God commands, loves, comforts, and judges in a manner consistent with himself and according to the covenant relationships that he establishes with his creatures. Indeed, as we move through redemptive history, God discloses himself not merely as unipersonal but as tripersonal, a being-in-relation, a unity of three persons: Father, Son, and Spirit (e.g.,

---

3. See John M. Frame, *The Doctrine of God*, Theology of Lordship (Phillipsburg, NJ: P&R, 2002), 1–115.

Matt. 28:18–20; John 1:1–4, 14–18; 5:16–30; 17:1–5; 1 Cor. 8:5–6; 2 Cor. 13:14; Eph. 1:3–14).

God is also the Holy One (Gen. 2:1–3; Ex. 3:2–5; Lev. 11:44; Isa. 6:1–3; cf. Rom. 1:18–23). God's holiness means more than his being "set apart." God's holiness is particularly associated with his independence, sovereignty, and glorious majesty.[4] As God, he is self-sufficient metaphysically and morally, and as such is categorically different in nature and existence from his creation; he shares his glory with no one (Isa. 40–48). God's holiness entails his personal-moral perfection. He is "of purer eyes than to see evil / and cannot look at wrong" (Hab. 1:13; cf. Isa. 1:4–20; 35:8). God *must* act with holy justice when his people rebel against him, yet he is the God who loves his people with a holy, covenant love (Hos. 11:9). God's holiness and love are never at odds (1 John 4:8; Rev. 4:8). Yet as sin enters the world and God graciously promises to redeem us, a question arises as to how he will do so and remain true to himself—but more on this below.

This summary of God's identity is the first truth, or building block, that helps us make sense of Christ's identity. God's nature as the triune Creator–covenant Lord gives a specific theistic shape to Scripture's interpretive framework, which in turn gives a specific theistic shape to Christ's identity. To help make this point, let's consider three specific examples.

First, the *triune nature of God* shapes Christ's identity. As we will see in chapter 3, Jesus views himself as the divine Son who even as incarnate continues to relate to the Father and the Spirit because they share fully and equally the one divine nature in perfect love and communion (John 1:1, 18; 17:5). In

---

4. See Willem VanGemeren, *New International Dictionary of Old Testament Theology and Exegesis*, 3 vols. (Grand Rapids, MI: Zondervan, 1997), 3:879; Richard A. Muller, *The Divine Essence and Attributes*, vol. 3 of *Post-Reformation Reformed Dogmatics* (Grand Rapids, MI: Baker Academic, 2003), 497–503.

fact, it's because Jesus is the Son that he is God, which in turn establishes his uniqueness and explains why his life and death have universal significance. Also, Jesus's actions and work cannot be understood apart from the relations of persons within the Trinity. After all, it's the Son who becomes flesh (John 1:14), not the Father or the Spirit, yet all three persons inseparably act in the incarnation and in all Jesus's works. Jesus, as the Son, acts from the Father and by the Spirit (John 1:32–34; 5:19–23). The Father sends the Son (John 3:16), the Spirit attends his union with human nature (Luke 1:35–37), and the Son redeems his people by the Spirit (Heb. 9:14). In every action, Jesus, as the incarnate Son, lived and died in unbroken unity with the Father and the Spirit. Christ is not a third party acting independently of God. Even at the cross, we see not three parties but only two: the triune God in and through the incarnate Son *and* humanity. The cross is a demonstration of the Father's love (John 3:16) by the gift of his Son.[5]

Second, the *covenantal character* of the triune God also shapes Christ's identity. By *covenantal*, I am first referring to what Reformed theology has called the "covenant of redemption," not the biblical covenants in history. Scripture teaches that God has an eternal plan (e.g., Ps. 139:16; Isa. 22:11; Eph. 1:4; 3:11; 2 Tim. 1:9; 1 Pet. 1:20). In that plan, the divine Son, consistent with the relations of persons within the Trinity, is appointed as the mediator of his people. The Son gladly and voluntarily accepts this appointment with its covenant stipulations and promises that are worked out in his incarnation, life, and cross work (Luke 24:25–27; Eph. 1:9–10; Heb. 10:5–7; Rev. 13:8). God's plan establishes why there is an incarnation (Heb. 2:5–18) and that the Son's role in that plan is to be a

---

5. On this point, see John R. W. Stott, *The Cross of Christ*, 20th anniversary ed. (Downers Grove, IL: InterVarsity Press, 2006), 133–62.

mediator, thus giving meaning and significance to Christ's person and work for us. We cannot understand Jesus's coming and work in the Gospels apart from it being the fulfillment of God's eternal plan and thus a *divine* work. Even in his human obedience, Jesus, as the Son, does the work that only God can do by inaugurating *God's* kingdom via his new covenant work (Heb. 9:15–10:18).

Third, the *lordship* of God also shapes Christ's identity. Theologians have captured the majestic sense of God's lordship with the term *aseity*—literally, "from oneself." But as John Frame reminds us, God's aseity is more than a metaphysical concept; it also has epistemological and ethical implications.[6] God is not only self-existent; he is also self-attesting (his omniscience is only from himself) and self-justifying (his will and nature are the moral standard).

Why is this significant for understanding who Christ is? First, as I discuss in chapter 4, the New Testament repeatedly presents Jesus as Yahweh by calling him "Lord," thus identifying him with the one true and living God (e.g., Rom. 10:9; 1 Cor. 12:3; Phil. 2:11). In biblical thought, no creature can share the attributes of God (Col. 2:9), carry out the works of God (Col. 1:15–20; Heb. 1:1–3), receive the worship of God (John 5:22–23; Phil. 2:9–11; Heb. 1:6; Rev. 5:11–12), and bear the titles and name of God (John 1:1, 18; 8:58; 20:28; Rom. 9:5; Phil. 2:9–11; Heb. 1:8–9) unless he is equal with God and thus one who shares the one, identical divine nature.[7]

Second, given that God's will and nature are the moral standard, then sin before this God is a serious problem. As the Holy One, God is "the Judge of all the earth" who always does what

---

6. Frame, *Doctrine of God*, 602.

7. On this point, see Richard Bauckham, *Jesus and the God of Israel: "God Crucified" and Other Studies on the New Testament's Christology of Divine Identity* (Grand Rapids, MI: Eerdmans, 2008).

is right (Gen. 18:25). But in promising to justify us before him (Gen. 15:6; Rom. 4:5), God cannot overlook our sin; he must remain true to his own righteous demands against sin. But how can God remain both just and the justifier of the ungodly? In Scripture, this is the major question that drives the Bible's entire redemptive storyline. Ultimately, as God's plan unfolds, this question is answered in a specific person, namely, Christ Jesus, who alone can redeem us precisely because he is the divine Son, who became human to act as our representative and substitute (Rom. 3:21–26). As God, he is able to satisfy his own righteous demands against us, and as human, he is able to satisfy the demands of covenant life for us as our new covenant head.

With just these three examples, we see how the identity of God functions to make sense of Christ's identity and why the divine Son had to become human to redeem us. We develop these connections in subsequent chapters, but our main point now is this: to know who Christ is, we must first think rightly about who God is.

The Requirement of Covenant Obedience

Making sense of the incarnation and why God the Son became man to save us from our sins (Matt. 1:21) requires a second building block: the nature of humans as image-sons (i.e., image bearers who are "sons" and thus represent God) and covenant creatures. To make sense of this point, however, requires that we go back to Adam and creation and then trace the Bible's link between the command and curse of the first Adam and the incarnation and work of the divine Son as the last Adam, which is the first Adam's only remedy.

Scripture divides the human race as falling under two representative heads: the first Adam and the last Adam (Rom. 5:12–21; 1 Cor. 15:12–28). In God's plan, Adam is a type of

Christ who anticipates the last Adam. Adam is not only the first man but also the covenant head and representative of all humanity. Adam's headship defines what it means to be human, and sadly, by his representative-legal act of disobedience, he plunges all people into sin (Rom. 5:12–21; cf. 3:23).

Central to God's relationship with humanity is his demand of covenantal obedience. After all, what else would our Creator–covenant Lord demand from us? Adam, as a creature of God and our covenant head, was called to covenant loyalty and complete obedience (Gen. 2:15–17). The tree of the knowledge of good and evil functions to test whether Adam will be an obedient image-son. Sadly, Adam disobeys, and the consequence of his action is not private. Postfall, all people are born "in Adam"—guilty and corrupt—and, sadly, continue to act in sin. Also, Adam's sin infects the entire creation; we now live in a fallen, abnormal, cursed world that only God can remedy (Rom. 8:18–25). The tree of life holds out an implied promise of life. Because of sin, however, Adam is expelled from Eden as God's act of judgment. Yet there is a glimmer of hope that we see in God's promise of Genesis 3:15 and the unfolding covenants.

Why is this important for understanding Christ? This building block gives the rationale for why the divine Son must become incarnate for us and why he must be greater. To undo and pay for Adam's sin, a "seed" of the woman (Gen. 3:15 ESV mg.) must come. In other words, for redemption to occur, a human must do it. *He* must render the required covenantal obedience God demands from us as a greater Adam. Yet the reversal of Adam's sin and all its disastrous effects will require more than a mere man. It will also require the divine Son, the true image of God (Col. 1:15; Heb. 1:3), to do the work of God, namely, remove the curse, pay for our sin, and usher in a new creation. To underscore why the reversal of Adam's sin will require more than a mere human, we need to turn to the next building block of Christ's identity.

The Nature of the Human Problem

Central to the covenant and the purpose of our creation is that our triune God has created humans to know him and to be his image-sons to display his glory and to expand the borders of Eden to the uttermost parts of the world.[8] But what happens when humans rebel against God, deface the image, and don't act as sons? Can the divine purpose still be accomplished? How is covenant peace possible without covenant obedience? How will God forgive those who sin against him?

The storyline from Genesis 3 forward reveals that Adam's disobedience brought sin into the world and humans under God's wrath. In Genesis 1:31, "God saw everything that he had made, and behold, it was very good." In Genesis 3, God expels Adam and Eve from his presence because of sin, and the transmission of sin is universal. By Genesis 6, human sin has so multiplied that it results in judgment by flood. Looking back on the course of human history, Paul confirms our universal fallenness: "None is righteous, no, not one. . . . For all have sinned and fall short of the glory of God" (Rom. 3:10, 23). Adam's sin turned the created order upside down and brought on us the sentence of death (Rom. 6:23). We were made to know, love, and serve God. But now we live under his righteous condemnation as his enemies and as objects of his wrath (Eph. 2:1–3).

What is God's response to our sin? Judgment and wrath, yet given God's promise to redeem, there is now what John

---

8. See G. K. Beale and Mitchell Kim, *God Dwells among Us: Expanding Eden to the Ends of the Earth* (Downers Grove, IL: InterVarsity Press, 2014).

Stott calls the "problem of forgiveness."[9] What is this problem? Considering the divine response to human sin, it seems that God must do two things that appear to be mutually exclusive: punish *and* forgive our sin. On the one hand, God must punish sin because he is holy and just. On the other hand, God created and covenanted with us to glorify himself in the righteous rule of humans over creation, not in our destruction. The problem, however, goes deeper, into the nature of God himself.

As noted above, God is holy and just, sin is against him, and sin must be punished.[10] Why? It is because of who God is as the moral standard of the universe. All God's attributes are essential to him, including his holiness, righteousness, and justice. In regard to his justice, God is not like a human judge, who adjudicates laws external to him; God *is* the law. Our sin is not against an abstract principle or impersonal law, but it's always against God (Ps. 51:4). So for God to forgive us, he must remain true to himself, which is wondrously a good thing! That is why our forgiveness is possible only if the full satisfaction of his moral demand is met. But this raises a crucial question: Who is able to satisfy God's righteous demands other than God himself?

It is precisely the necessity that God judge human sin and his promise to redeem that together create a tension in the Bible's storyline and in covenantal relationships. God promises to be our God, but we are under the sentence of death. We cannot save ourselves; salvation must come from God (Jonah 2:9). But how and by whom? Scripture teaches that we need a representative substitute but not merely a human one. What is needed is the *divine* Son to become human and to do for us what we

---

9. Stott, *Cross of Christ*, 90–91.

10. This paragraph is adapted from Stephen J. Wellum, "Answering 4 Common Objections to Penal Substitutionary Atonement," 9Marks, https://www.9marks.org/article/answering-4-common-objections-to-psa/. Used by permission of 9Marks.

cannot do: obey for us and satisfy his own righteous demands against us.

With these three building blocks in place, we can better grasp Christ's identity and why he has come. First, because of who God is, he must provide his own solution to the problem of forgiving sin. Second, because God has created humans to rule over creation, salvation must come through a man. Third, because of the universal corruption of sin, this last Adam must be greater than the first and ultimately identified with God. Thus, from the Bible's storyline, the Redeemer to come must identify with God in his nature and with humanity in ours. To underscore this point from Scripture, let's turn to the fourth building block.

The Triune God Saves through the Obedience of God the Son[11]

Just as human sin and God's promise to redeem bring tension into the Bible's storyline, so the resolution of this tension raises the question of just who it is that is qualified to establish God's kingdom on earth and to save us from our sins. God created humans as his image-sons to rule over the world (Gen. 1:26–31; Ps. 8). Yet no one "in Adam" is able to do so. Who, then, is able to establish God's rule, to undo what Adam did by rendering perfect covenant obedience, and to pay for our sins before God? The answer: Jesus alone as God the Son incarnate.

The Bible teaches this truth by the unfolding of God's plan through the biblical covenants.[12] After Adam's sin, God does not leave us to ourselves. Instead, God acts in sovereign grace

---

11. This section is adapted from Stephen J. Wellum, "*Solus Christus*: What the Reformers Taught and Why It Still Matters," *Southern Baptist Journal of Theology* 19, no. 4 (2015): 79–107. Used by permission of *The Southern Baptist Journal of Theology*.

12. For a detailed treatment of the covenants, see Peter J. Gentry and Stephen J. Wellum, *Kingdom through Covenant: A Biblical-Theological Understanding of the Covenants*, 2nd ed. (Wheaton, IL: Crossway, 2018).

and promises to reverse the manifold effects of sin through his provision of a "seed" of the woman (Gen. 3:15 ESV mg.)—a promise that is given greater clarity over time. Although in embryonic form, we learn that this coming Redeemer will destroy the works of Satan and restore goodness to this world. This promise creates the expectation that when it is finally realized, sin and death will be destroyed, and the fullness of God's saving reign will come. As God's plan unfolds, we discover who this Redeemer is and how he will save us. We can develop this last point in three steps.

First, God's promise unfolds through the covenants with Noah, Abraham, Israel, and David. Step-by-step, God prepares his people to anticipate the coming of the "seed"—a person who will be human but also more. How? Scripture teaches that the fulfillment of God's promises will be *through a human*, anticipated by various typological persons such as Adam, Noah, Moses, Israel, and David. But Scripture also identifies this "anointed one" (messiah) *with God*. How so? Scripture records what this messiah-king does: he inaugurates God's kingdom, shares God's throne, and does what only God can do (e.g., Pss. 2; 45; 110; Isa. 9:6–7; Ezek. 34).

Second, how does God's kingdom come in its *redemptive–new creation* sense (Isa. 65:17)? Over time, God's saving kingdom is revealed and, at least in anticipatory form, comes to this world through the covenant mediators—Adam, Noah, Abraham and his seed, Israel, and, most significantly, David and his sons. Yet the Old Testament repeatedly reminds us that none of these covenant heads are the one. This is particularly emphasized with the Davidic kings, who are "sons" to Yahweh, the representatives of Israel, and who are to bring God's rule to this world (2 Sam. 7:14, 19; Pss. 2; 72; 110; Isa. 11; 52:13–55:13). Yet David and his sons ultimately point forward to the coming of David's greater Son, who truly obeys and inaugurates God's saving reign through the ratification of a new covenant and all that it signifies.

In this regard, Jeremiah 31 is probably the most famous new covenant text in the Old Testament, although teaching on the new covenant is found in all the Prophets. As the Prophets anticipate the new covenant, they link it to the coming of David's greater Son, the work of the Spirit (Isa. 11; Ezek. 36:25–27; Joel 2:28–32), the new creation (Isa. 65:17), and God's saving work among the nations.[13] But Jeremiah focuses on what is truly central to the new covenant, namely, the promise of the complete forgiveness of sin (Jer. 31:34). Under the Mosaic covenant, forgiveness of sin was normally granted via the sacrificial system. God, however, never intended for the old system to be an end in itself. This is why God announces that in the new covenant, sin will be remembered "no more" (Jer. 31:34), which entails the full payment of it. Thus, under the new covenant what is anticipated is the perfect fellowship of God and his people and the dwelling of God with us in a new creation—ultimately the fulfillment of Genesis 3:15.

Third, we can now take the Bible's covenantal storyline and see how it identifies who Christ is. If we step back and ask, Who is able to fulfill all God's promises, inaugurate his saving rule in this world, and achieve the full forgiveness of sin? The answer: *God alone.*

Isn't this what the Old Testament teaches? As the Scripture traces the history of Israel, it becomes evident that God alone must act unilaterally to keep his promises to redeem. After all, who can usher in the new creation, final judgment, and salvation? Who can forgive sin but God alone? Certainly, God's promises are fulfilled not by the previous covenant mediators,

---

13. On this point, see Gentry and Wellum, *Kingdom through Covenant*, 487–765.

nor by the nation of Israel, for they have all, in different ways, disobeyed and come under judgment. If there is to be salvation at all, God must do it. But as the covenants teach, God has promised to save through another David—a human—yet one who is also identified with Yahweh.

It is this basic storyline that serves as the scaffolding for the New Testament's presentation of Jesus.[14] Who is Jesus? According to Scripture, he is the one who inaugurates God's kingdom and new covenant age, which results in the full forgiveness of sin. In him, the eschatological Spirit is poured out, the new creation dawns, and all God's promises are fulfilled. But in light of the Old Testament, who can do such a thing? Scripture answers: the only one who can do it is the obedient image-son-priest-king—a greater Adam—who is also identified with Yahweh.

As Jesus arrives on the scene, this is precisely how the New Testament presents him. In Christ Jesus, all the Law and the Prophets are fulfilled (Matt. 5:17). In him, we see the resolution of God to take on himself our sin and guilt in order to reverse the horrible effects of the fall and to satisfy his own righteous requirements, to make this world right, and to inaugurate a new covenant in his blood (Rom. 3:21–26; 5:1–8:39; 1 Cor. 15:1–34; Eph. 1:7–10; Heb. 8). In Jesus Christ, we see the perfectly obedient Son, who is also the Lord, taking the initiative to keep his covenant promises by becoming human, veiling his glory, and securing our redemption (Phil. 2:6–11; Heb. 2:5–18; 9:11–10:18). In Christ, Old Testament eschatological expectations unite: he is Yahweh who saves and David's greater Son (Isa. 9:6–7; 11; Jer. 23:1–6; Ezek. 34). In this way, the Bible's storyline through the covenants not only anticipates Jesus's

---

14. This and the following paragraph are adapted from Stephen J. Wellum, "Christological Reflections in Light of Scripture's Covenants," *Southern Baptist Journal of Theology* 16, no. 2 (2012): 79–107. Used by permission of *The Southern Baptist Journal of Theology*.

coming but also identifies him as God the Son incarnate, fully God and fully man.

This is a good reminder that to know who Jesus is, we must know him from the entire Bible. Again, Jesus does not come to us in a vacuum but within the Bible's storyline, framework, and categories. In this chapter, we have sought to establish some of those foundational building blocks to grasp who Jesus is, what he has come to do, and why he is unique. In the next two chapters, we turn to the New Testament to establish further that all Scripture consistently teaches what the church has come to confess: Jesus is God the Son incarnate.

3

Who Does Jesus
Say That He Is?

The Bible's covenantal storyline serves as the metanarrative to identify who Jesus is and as the background to the New Testament's presentation of him.[1] Who is Jesus? According to Scripture, he is the one who inaugurates God's kingdom and the new covenant age. In him, the full forgiveness of sin is achieved, the eschatological Spirit is poured out, the new creation dawns, and all God's promises reach their fulfillment. But this raises an important question: Who can do this? Scripture answers: the only one who can do it is both Yahweh (Lord) and the obedient human Son, and the New Testament presents Jesus in precisely this way.

But did Jesus know himself to be God the Son incarnate? Did Jesus self-identify as the eternal Son of the Father, the promised human Messiah, who came to reveal the Father, do the

---

1. This paragraph is adapted from Stephen J. Wellum, "Christological Reflections in Light of Scripture's Covenants," *Southern Baptist Journal of Theology* 16, no. 2 (2012): 79–107. Used by permission of *The Southern Baptist Journal of Theology*.

works of God, and by so doing, demonstrate that he is God the Son? These are not easy questions to answer. On the one hand, Scripture teaches that Jesus was born, "increased in wisdom and in stature" (Luke 2:52), and did not know certain things (Matt. 24:36). This reality reveals that Jesus is fully human, the promised "seed" of the woman (Gen. 3:15 ESV mg.), and thus able to act as our covenant head and Redeemer. On the other hand, Jesus's self-understanding is that he is more than merely a human image-son; he is also the divine Son. In this chapter, our focus is on the latter point, without minimizing the former. We look at the implicit and explicit witness of Jesus to his own identity, set within the Bible's storyline and interpretive framework. In part 2, we address how the church's theologizing about Christ carefully maintained both truths.

The Implicit Witness of Christ

Jesus's entire life testified to who he thought he was. But our focus is on five important aspects of his earthly life that reveal his self-identity to be the divine Son: his baptism, his life and ministry, his death and resurrection, the worship he received, and his inauguration of the kingdom.

Baptism

Jesus comes to John the Baptist and the Jordan not accidentally but with the intent "to fulfill all righteousness" (Matt. 3:15). And upon his baptism, the Holy Spirit descends on him, and the Father addresses him as his beloved Son (Matt. 3:16–17). From the Bible's storyline, Jesus knows that to have the Spirit from the Father signals that he is the promised Messiah who inaugurates God's kingdom (Isa. 61:1–2; Luke 4:16–21; see Ezek. 34).[2] But

---

2. On this point, see Thomas R. Schreiner, *New Testament Theology: Magnifying God in Christ* (Grand Rapids, MI: Baker Academic, 2008), 172–73; D. A. Carson, *Mat-*

to be the Spirit-anointed Messiah who fulfills the prophetic expectation of redemption, restoration, and new creation is also to be identified with Yahweh, since it is only God who can do such a work (Ps. 110; Isa. 9:6–7).

This truth is underscored in the Father's statement "This is my beloved Son" (Matt. 3:17, a combination of Ps. 2:7 and Isa. 42:1). These texts confirm that Jesus is the son-king who ushers in God's saving reign.[3] How? In the framework of the Old Testament, the Father's address does not simply mean that Jesus is the promised Davidic priest-son-king (although he is!) but also that he is the divine Son of the Father and that he alone can do the work of God.

Life and Ministry

Throughout his life and ministry, Jesus understands himself to be the Son in unique relation to his Father and the only man to share the authority and power of God himself. How early does Jesus know this? The Gospels don't say, since they record little of Jesus's first thirty years, yet he seems to know this as early as twelve years old (Luke 2:49–50). As for Jesus's public ministry, however, Matthew captures it in terms of Jesus's teaching and miracles. In fact, on two occasions, we are told that Jesus goes "throughout all Galilee, teaching in their synagogues and proclaiming the gospel of the kingdom and healing every disease and every affliction among the people" (Matt. 4:23; see 9:35). In the narrative, these two verses function as bookends to encapsulate Jesus's ministry up to his death.[4]

Why is this significant? Jesus's teaching (Matt. 5–7) and miracles (Matt. 8–9) are not merely like that of Moses or Elijah,

thew, in vol. 8 of *The Expositor's Bible Commentary* (Grand Rapids, MI: Zondervan, 1984), 106–10.

3. See Carson, *Matthew*, 106–10; Schreiner, *New Testament Theology*, 172–73.

4. See Murray J. Harris, *Three Crucial Questions about Jesus* (Grand Rapids, MI: Baker, 1994), 82–83.

who were specially endowed by the Spirit. No doubt, Jesus's Spirit endowment fulfills the pattern of previous prophets, priests, and kings, yet it's more. Jesus's ministry is placed in the context of the inauguration of God's kingdom, which entails that Jesus shares the authority of God. No previous leader ever inaugurated God's promised kingdom; Jesus is simply in a different category, and he knows it.

Consider how Jesus views his own teaching authority and miracles as evidence that he has inaugurated God's supernatural reign. Jesus claims that all the Law and Prophets are fulfilled in him (Matt. 5:17–20; 11:11–15). This assertion is staggering. Jesus sees himself as the eschatological goal of God's entire revelation and its sole authoritative interpreter.[5] This is nothing less than a claim to share God's authority as the divine Son.

Or consider Jesus's miracles, which bear witness to his unique relation to the Father. In fact, Jesus's healing and nature miracles display the authority and power of God. Jesus's healing miracles reveal God's promised kingdom and the arrival of the messianic age (Luke 7:22–23; see Isa. 29:18–19; 35:5–6; 61:1). Jesus's authority and power over nature—for example, calming the stormy sea by his command (Matt. 8:26) and walking on water (Matt. 14:25, 28–30)—are significant, especially when placed in the Bible's storyline and not viewed in isolation. In the Old Testament, Yahweh reveals that he alone triumphs over the stormy sea (see Pss. 65:7; 107:23–31) and treads on its waters (Job 9:8 LXX; see Ps. 77:19; Isa. 51:9–10).[6] In a similar manner, the New Testament presents Jesus's miracles and exorcism of demons (Matt. 4:23; 9:35; 10:7–8; Luke 9:11; 10:9, 17; 11:20) as evidence that Jesus has the authority and power of

---

5. See Carson, *Matthew*, 140–47.

6. On this point, see Simon J. Gathercole, *The Preexistent Son: Recovering the Christologies of Matthew, Mark, and Luke* (Grand Rapids, MI: Eerdmans, 2006), 64.

God. This is why Jesus's miracles implicitly identify him with Yahweh by doing what God alone can do.[7]

Furthermore, Jesus exercises God's authority and power through forgiveness of sins, judgment, and resurrection. In light of the fall, humanity's greatest problem is sin before a holy and righteous God. Ultimately, God is the only one with the authority to forgive sin, because sin first and foremost is against him. In fact, at the heart of the "newness" of the new covenant is the promise of the full forgiveness of sin (Jer. 31:34). In a statement of staggering importance, Jesus claims that he has God's authority to forgive sins when he says to the paralytic, "Son, your sins are forgiven" (Mark 2:5; cf. 2:10). In addition, the Prophets predicted that God's kingdom and future age would contain the hope of resurrection life (Ezek. 37:1–23; Dan. 12:2)—all works of God alone. Jesus announces that the Father has appointed him, as the Son, to exercise divine judgment and to give resurrection life (Matt. 7:22–23; John 5:19–30; 11:25–26)—thus self-identifying with God in his authority and work.

Death and Resurrection

Jesus also self-identifies as the divine Son incarnate in his death and resurrection. As Jesus approaches his death, he does not view it as martyrdom; instead, it is central to his divinely planned messianic mission (Matt. 16:21–23). He repeatedly explains that he *must* (Gk. *dei*) die and then be raised. Jesus knows that he will die, and he embraces his death in love for his Father and as a willing, obedient act to fulfill God's eternal plan (Mark 10:45; Luke 18:31; John 10:17–18).

---

7. Contra Gerald Hawthorne et al., who teach that Jesus did most or all of his miracles by the Spirit's power and that Jesus's miracles are thus not evidence of his deity. See Gerald F. Hawthorne, *The Presence and the Power: The Significance of the Holy Spirit in the Life and Ministry of Jesus* (repr., Eugene, OR: Wipf and Stock, 2003); Fred Sanders and Klaus D. Issler, eds., *Jesus in Trinitarian Perspective* (Nashville: B&H Academic, 2007), 114–53; 189–225.

In light of the Old Testament, Jesus knows that his death will bring divine judgment on the world because he is the Son (John 12:30–33) and will reconcile God and man because he has authority on earth to forgive sins (Mark 2:5–12). David Wells sums up the identifying power of Jesus's death and resurrection with a rhetorical question: "His actions, in this regard, had an implied Christological significance, for who can forgive sin but God alone? (Mark 2:7 / Luke 5:21)."[8]

Praise and Worship

In a biblical worldview, God alone is worthy of worship, he shares his glory with no one, and he rightly demands worship and total devotion from his creatures. To worship any created thing rather than God is idolatry (see Acts 14:14–15; Rom. 1:18–23; Rev. 5:9–14; 19:10).

What is crucial to note, however, is that Jesus receives human worship and never rebukes people for giving it (Matt. 14:33; 21:15–16; 28:9, 17; John 20:28).[9] But Jesus raises the significance of this veneration a notch. Knowing that his Father has committed all authority to him, Jesus explains why he has done so: "that all may honor the Son, just as they honor the Father. Whoever does not honor the Son does not honor the Father who sent him" (John 5:23). Jesus, then, receives the worship that only God is to receive and also demands it, precisely because he self-identifies with God as his Son.

Inauguration of God's Kingdom

We now come full circle. The Gospels, especially the Synoptics, view Christ's entire life and ministry in terms of his inau-

---

8. David F. Wells, *The Person of Christ: A Biblical and Historical Analysis of the Incarnation* (Westchester, IL: Crossway, 1984), 41.

9. On this point, see Larry W. Hurtado, *Lord Jesus Christ: Devotion to Jesus in Earliest Christianity* (Grand Rapid, MI: Eerdmans, 2003).

guration of God's kingdom. Whether it's in Jesus's baptism, teaching, miracles, or death and resurrection, it's all evidence that the prophetic "age to come" is now here in him. But in Old Testament thought, the coming of God's kingdom not only comes *through* the Davidic king—a son-king to Yahweh, or the Father (2 Sam. 7:14)—but is also an act of *God* to restore his people, to forgive sin, and to usher in a new creation. In this way, the human son-king is also identified with God. Significantly, Jesus claims that *he* inaugurates this kingdom.

In fact, much of Jesus's implicit witness to himself depends on this unavoidable deduction: if the works that Jesus does can be accomplished only by God, then by performing these works, the man Jesus implies that he, as the Son, shares the same authority as God his Father. Thus, in every aspect of his life, in every word he speaks, and in every work he performs, Jesus views himself as the Son of the Father, fulfilling the plan of the Creator–covenant Lord to redeem a people for himself and to reign over his creation in perfect righteousness.[10]

Although Jesus never says, "I am God the Son incarnate," he implicitly self-identifies as such. We cannot think of Jesus's words and works isolated from their place in the Bible's storyline and interpretive framework. Jesus knows that he is the one to accomplish *God's* plan, to do *God's* works, and to receive *God's* worship. As such, Jesus knows himself to be God the Son incarnate.

The Explicit Witness of Christ

In addition to Jesus's implicit witness regarding himself, we also have explicit statements that reveal his self-identity as the divine Son, who is also the human son, in relation to his Father.

---

10. See Wells, *Person of Christ*, 38.

Use of Abba

Jesus addresses God by the Aramaic term *Abba*, which reveals how he perceives his relationship to the Father: it is singular and unique (Matt. 6:9; 11:25–26).[11] When Jesus teaches his disciples how to address God, he teaches them to pray, "Our Father" (Matt. 6:9; John 20:17). But Jesus views his relationship to his Father as unique. We call God *Abba* as adopted sons because of Jesus's work and our covenant union with him (see Rom. 8:15; Gal. 4:6). Jesus's use of the term, however, is due to his unique relationship to his Father—he is the eternal Son (John 1:1; 5:19–30; 17:5).

Son of God[12]

Jesus as the eternal Son is reinforced by the title—indeed, name—Son of God. The title appears in the Synoptic Gospels and occupies a central place in John's Gospel (John 3:16; 5:19–23). It is applied to Jesus at his baptism (Mark 1:11), temptation (Luke 4:9), and transfiguration (Mark 9:7). In John, the title is so central to Christ's identity that John writes the Gospel "so that [his readers] may believe that Jesus is the Christ, the Son of God" (John 20:31).

Once again, to grasp the significance of what Jesus means by self-identifying as God's Son, we must think in terms of the Old Testament. First, *son* is closely identified with *image of God*, and as such, it is applied to key typological figures: Adam (Luke 3:38), Israel (Ex. 4:22–23), and the Davidic king (2 Sam. 7:14), who are to represent God. Building on this pattern, Jesus is the true son, namely, the human son, who

---

11. See Joachim Jeremias, *The Prayers of Jesus* (Philadelphia: Fortress, 1989).

12. For a detailed treatment of the title Son, see D. A. Carson, *Jesus the Son of God: A Christological Title Often Overlooked, Sometimes Misunderstood, and Currently Disputed* (Wheaton, IL: Crossway, 2012); Graeme Goldsworthy, *The Son of God and the New Creation*, Short Studies in Biblical Theology (Wheaton, IL: Crossway, 2015).

fulfills the role of previous sons but who is greater (Rom. 1:3–4; Phil. 2:6–11).

Jesus's incarnational sonship, however, is not the whole story. Already in the Old Testament we learn that David's greater Son takes on the identity of Yahweh. From this we discover that Jesus's sonship is more than being a mere human; he is also the eternal Son, the true image and exact representation of the Father (Col. 1:15–17; Heb. 1:2–3), and thus united as one with the Father and disclosing in time something of God's eternal, intra-Trinitarian divine life.

This truth is underscored by Jesus himself. As noted, Jesus regularly addresses God as *Abba*, or "Father" (Matt. 11:25; 16:17; Luke 23:46). These expressions go beyond a mere human relationship. As a child, Jesus tells his earthly parents of his unique Son-Father relationship (Luke 2:49). Before his death, Jesus speaks of his eternal sonship: "And now, Father, glorify me in your own presence with the glory that I had with you before the world existed" (John 17:5). Not only does Jesus know that he is appointed to be the Son in his incarnate life, he also knows that he has always been the eternal Son. John 5:16–20 and Matthew 11:25–27 prove this point.

In John 5, after healing a crippled man, Jesus responds to those who criticize him for working on the Sabbath: "My Father is working until now, and I am working" (John 5:17). In so doing, Jesus not only calls God his own Father, he also makes himself equal with God by claiming the same authority as God to work on the Sabbath. And in the following verses, Jesus explains that the validity of his Sabbath work is based on the divine nature of all his works (specifically judgment and resurrection), the divine worship warranted by these works (John 5:22–23), and the divine aseity (John 5:26) of the one who performs these works. Who does Jesus think he is? He views himself as the eternal Son who shares with the Father the divine nature and thus has the right and authority to do all that God does.

Jesus also speaks of his divine sonship in Matthew 11:25–27, this time in terms of mutual knowledge and shared sovereignty with the Father—an explicit claim to deity. Yet Jesus's divine self-identity does not contradict his self-identity as the human son. Both must be affirmed.

Son of Man

Jesus also testifies to his identity as God the Son incarnate by his most common self-designation, the Son of Man. The title is used in the Gospels and always by Jesus himself. Again, to grasp what Jesus means by the title, it's crucial to understand it within its Old Testament background.[13]

No doubt, the title refers to Jesus's humanity. In the Old Testament, "son of man" is used as a synonym for humans in the context of our role in creation (Ps. 8:4). But in Daniel 7, "son of man" takes on the significance of a superhuman figure who functions alongside the "Ancient of Days," that is, Yahweh. In Daniel's vision, God gives his kingdom to "one like a son of man" (Dan. 7:13–14). But *this* son of man is different from all others: he comes on the "clouds of heaven," his reign lasts forever, and his reign gives dominion over the whole earth to his kingdom people (Dan. 7:13–14, 18, 22, 27), thus identifying him with God. So, *this* son of man is the promised son-king, who, because he is both God and human, will bring reconciliation between God and humans and restore our righteous vice-regent rule over God's creation.

When Jesus steps into this biblical storyline as the self-designated Son of Man, he makes an astounding claim regarding his identity. As the Son of Man, Jesus identifies as both God

---

13. See Schreiner, *New Testament Theology*, 213–31; C. F. D. Moule, *The Origin of Christology* (Cambridge: Cambridge University Press, 1977), 11–22.

and man. Jesus uses the title in his humiliation as a man to save the lost (Matt. 8:20; Mark 10:45), in his divine authority to forgive sins (Mark 2:10), and in his divine power to resurrect the dead (Matt. 17:9). And Jesus also refers to himself as the Son of Man in his resurrected-incarnational ascension to the throne of heaven (Matt. 19:28) and in his foretelling of his future return as the king of heaven, "coming on the clouds of heaven with power and great glory" (Matt. 24:30).

Divine Purpose and Work

Jesus also identifies as God the Son incarnate in the purpose of his coming. On numerous occasions, Jesus offers "I have come to" statements, in which he reveals why he has come.

For example, Jesus declares that he has come to preach the good news of the kingdom (Mark 1:38), to fulfill the Law and the Prophets (Matt. 5:17), to call sinners to himself (Matt. 9:13), and so on. In each case, Jesus understands his own identity in divine terms.[14] Even more explicit is Jesus's self-identity as the one who forgives sins (Mark 2:1–12). The religious leaders correctly assert that God alone forgives sins. But they fail to see that Jesus is the divine Son and that the promised forgiveness of sin and covenantal reconciliation between God and humans are fulfilled in Jesus. In him, Immanuel, "God with us," is here (Matt. 1:21–23; cf. Jer. 31:34).[15] The temple, priesthood, and sacrificial system played their typological function to set the stage for God himself to come as the man Jesus to achieve our eternal redemption.

"I Am"

Alongside the purpose statements in the Synoptics, John's Gospel gives us the famous "I am" (Gk. *egō eimi*) statements by

---

14. On this point, see Gathercole, *Preexistent Son*, 83–189.
15. See Carson, *Matthew*, 222.

which Jesus self-identifies with God. When Jesus refers to himself as "I am" without a predicate (John 6:20; 8:24, 28, 58; 18:5, 6, 8), he links his personal identity with the unique, personal name of Yahweh, the Creator–covenant Lord (Ex. 3:6, 14). It's as if Jesus has stepped into the Old Testament storyline and explicitly called himself God.

For example, in John 8, Jesus concludes another controversy with the Jews regarding his origin and identity by declaring, "Truly, truly, I say to you, before Abraham was, I am" (John 8:58). The Jewish leaders are clinging to their descent from Abraham. But Jesus explicitly refers to himself as "I am" to reveal himself to be the God of Abraham. Another example is John 13:19. As Tom Schreiner rightly notes, "The use of 'I am' demonstrates that such predictions are not merely the prophecies of an ordinary prophet. Jesus demonstrates his deity by proclaiming what will happen before it occurs."[16] Even more, Jesus knows that he has existed as the Son in an eternal relation with his Father when he prays, "Father, glorify me in your own presence with the glory that I had with you before the world existed" (John 17:5). All this data points to the fact that Jesus knows that he has been one with the Father from eternity and thus is the divine Son.

In addition, Jesus also identifies with Yahweh by referring to himself as the typological fulfillment of various Old Testament persons, events, and institutions. For example, in John 10:11, Jesus says, "I am the good shepherd." By using this predicate within the plotline of Scripture, Jesus is not only claiming to fulfill the role of Israel's kings to shepherd the people while all those kings failed (Ezek. 34:1–9), he is also identifying himself with God (Ps. 23; Ezek. 34:11–13). Thus, in all Jesus's "I am" sayings, he explicitly identifies as God the Son incarnate.

---

16. Schreiner, *New Testament Theology*, 253.

Our Object of Faith

Finally, Jesus explicitly makes himself the object of saving faith that is reserved for God alone. Repeatedly, the Old Testament teaches that "salvation belongs to the Lord!" (Jonah 2:9). The New Testament doesn't contradict this truth, but it now makes Jesus the proper object of saving faith (see John 12:44; 14:1; Acts 16:34; Rom. 4:3, 5, 17, 24; Gal. 3:6; 1 Thess. 1:8; Titus 3:8; Heb. 6:1; 1 Pet. 1:21).[17]

This shift to Jesus does *not* mean that he is a rival object of faith. Instead, it entails that Jesus, as the Son, is deity yet distinct from the Father. Within the Bible's covenantal storyline, which Jesus knows well, he can confidently center his disciples' faith in him precisely because he knows he is the divine Son. No doubt, the New Testament presents Jesus as a model of faith for us, but before we can model our faith after Jesus, Scripture commands us to trust him as the object of our faith, as the God of our salvation. As the apostles testify in light of the advent of Christ, "There is no other name under heaven given among men by which we must be saved" (Acts 4:12; see also Acts 10:43; 16:31; Rom. 10:9–11; 1 Cor. 1:2; 1 John 3:23; 5:13).

Did Jesus know himself to be God the Son incarnate? The answer to this question is yes.[18] This in no way minimizes Christ's true humanity and the fact that he "increased in wisdom and in stature" (Luke 2:52). Yet Scripture teaches that Jesus is more

---

17. See Harris, *Three Crucial Questions*, 77.

18. Our conclusion that Jesus self-identifies as God the Son incarnate differs from N. T. Wright. Wright has turned back unwarranted skepticism among biblical scholars regarding the historical Jesus, but he denies that Jesus knew he was God the Son; see N. T. Wright, *The Challenge of Jesus: Rediscovering Who Jesus Was and Is* (Downers Grove, IL: InterVarsity Press, 1999), 96–125. Wright contends that Jesus viewed himself as carrying out the vocation of Yahweh, yet awareness of vocation is not the same thing as Jesus knowing he is God the Son. Wright is often right, but his conclusion does not account for Jesus's self-identity in the biblical data we have examined, let alone the entire biblical storyline. Jesus views himself as the messianic "son" *and* the eternal Son who has come to fulfill his Father's will and to redeem God's people.

than a mere human; he is also the eternal Son of the Father, who has become human. By investigating Jesus's implicit and explicit words and works, we have discovered that Jesus knew that he was the Son who had come from heaven to do as a man on earth what only God could do. By making the specific claims he made, and doing the particular works he did at the precise point he came in the storyline of Scripture, Jesus made a clear claim: he is God the Son incarnate. It is for this reason that the church rightly confesses that Jesus is Lord, the Word made flesh for our salvation, and thus truly worthy of our faith, love, obedience, and worship.

4

The New Testament
Witness to Christ

In this chapter we continue to summarize the biblical data regarding who Jesus is as God the Son incarnate by turning to the apostolic witness to Christ. The apostles' understanding of Jesus's identity is no different from Jesus's self-identity; in fact, they learned it from him.

We cannot do an exhaustive survey of the biblical data.[1] Instead, our focus is on key texts that not only summarize the New Testament witness to Christ but also teach significant truths that are foundational for the church's later Christological formulation. It's crucial to see the continuity between what Scripture teaches and what the church confesses. The Jesus of the Bible is not different from the Jesus confessed in Nicene

---

1. See Richard Bauckham, *Jesus and the God of Israel: "God Crucified" and Other Studies on the New Testament's Christology of Divine Identity* (Grand Rapids, MI: Eerdmans, 2008); Robert Bowman Jr. and J. Ed Komoszewski, *Putting Jesus in His Place: The Case for the Deity of Christ* (Grand Rapids, MI: Kregel, 2007); Gordon D. Fee, *Pauline Christology: An Exegetical-Theological Study* (Peabody, MA: Hendrickson, 2007); Thomas R. Schreiner, *New Testament Theology: Magnifying God in Christ* (Grand Rapids, MI: Baker Academic, 2008), 305–38, 380–430.

and Chalcedonian orthodoxy, although a different theological vocabulary is used to faithfully communicate the biblical teaching.[2]

It is also important to see that the apostles present Jesus within the Bible's storyline. Jesus is first the promised Messiah, David's greater Son, who inaugurates God's saving rule and reign. Jesus is clearly a human son-king—first promised in Eden (Gen. 3:15), given definition through the covenants, epitomized in the Davidic king (e.g., Isa. 7:14; 9:6–7; 11; 52:13–53:12; Ezek. 34)—and the one who fulfills the role of previous sons (e.g., Adam, Israel, David). Yet this human son-king is not merely human; he is also the divine Son who alone does what God can do. This latter emphasis identifies the human Messiah with Yahweh in a unique Father-Son relationship that transcends the human, thus becoming the seedbed for Trinitarian reflection. Jesus, the Christ, is not merely human; he is also one with Yahweh: God the Son incarnate.

We turn now to some key Christological texts that summarize the apostolic teaching regarding Christ and on which the church faithfully formulates Christological orthodoxy.

John 1:1–18

I cannot overstate the importance of John's prologue for the entire Gospel and the New Testament. It reminds us that Jesus is the divine Word, the eternal Son of the Father, become human. In fact, these verses summarize, as D. A. Carson reminds us,

---

2. Why was such a theological vocabulary necessary? The church had to use extra-biblical language to communicate accurately and faithfully what Scripture taught about Jesus, especially in light of various false ways (i.e., heresies) of putting together the biblical data about Christ. Often the false ways of thinking about Christ merely repeated Scripture as if biblical texts required no explanation, but what was at dispute was the meaning of those texts in light of the Bible's entire presentation of Christ. The church, then, had to work carefully from biblical exegesis to theological understanding to account for and to explain all the scriptural teaching in the way that Scripture teaches it. For more on this point, see chap. 5.

how the "Word" which was with God in the very beginning came into the sphere of time, history, tangibility—in other words, how the Son of God was sent into the world to become the Jesus of history, so that the glory and grace of God might be uniquely and perfectly disclosed. The rest of the book is nothing other than an expansion of this theme.[3]

Indeed, the entire New Testament is likewise merely an expansion of this theme.

How does the prologue identify our Lord Jesus Christ as the divine Son who became human? It does so by its use of "Word" (Gk. *logos*) and "God" (Gk. *theos*). John is the only biblical author to identify Christ by the title Word. To establish its meaning, we need to locate the term within the Old Testament, instead of looking outside Scripture, despite its widespread use in Greek thought.[4] In the Old Testament, "Word" is closely associated with God, who creates, reveals, and redeems—all by his Word (Gen. 1:3–27; 3:8–19; 12:1; Pss. 33:6, 9; 119:9, 25; Isa. 55:11). By the use of this title, John identifies Jesus, the Son, with God. But further, by his use of "God," John also teaches that the Word *is* God yet is simultaneously *distinct from* God (the Father).

In John 1:1, John uses a triadic structure to make these points. Each of the three clauses has the same subject, "Word," and an identical verb, "was" (Gk. *ēn*), and each clause progresses to the next. The first clause, "In the beginning was the Word" (1:1a), teaches that the Word is eternal; hence Jesus as the Son is eternal. The second clause, "the Word was with God" (1:1b), affirms that although the Word is eternal, he is also distinct from God (the Father), hence affirming an eternal Father-Son relation. The

3. D. A. Carson, *The Gospel according to John*, Pillar New Testament Commentary (Grand Rapids, MI: Eerdmans, 1992), 111.
4. On this point, see Carson, *John*, 114–18.

last clause, "the Word was God" (1:1c), asserts that the Word shares the full deity of God.[5] Since there is only one Creator–covenant God, this entails that within God there is a Father-Son relation that shares the one divine nature—hence, John 1:1 is a foundational verse in the church's Trinitarian formulation. In this key verse, then, John declares that the Word has an eternal existence in personal intercommunion with God and that both share the same nature. And as John now explains, it is *this* Word, God's own self-expression—very God of God—who becomes human and is our Lord Jesus Christ (1:14).

Before we turn to John's teaching on the incarnation, however, it is significant that predicating "God" (Gk. *theos*) to Christ is not limited to John; this construction occurs at least seven times in the New Testament (John 1:1, 18; 20:28; Rom. 9:5; Titus 2:13; 2 Pet. 1:1; Heb. 1:8).[6] Why is this important? Scripture applies many titles to Christ, but most of them refer to Christ's deity *and* humanity—for example, "Son," "Son of Man," and "Messiah." But *theos* applies to Jesus as an explicit assertion that he is God. No doubt, the title "Lord" (Gk. *kyrios*) is similar, but *theos* is more explicit.

Why is "God" not used more often, given its clear affirmation of Christ's deity? Three reasons may be given. First, we should not forget that Scripture states that the Son is "God" at least *seven* times and in key places. In fact, four different authors state it (John, Paul, Peter, and the author of Hebrews), and they do so consistently—immediately after the resurrection (John 20:28), into the AD 90s (John 1:1, 18), and in both Jewish and

---

5. From the patristic era (Arius) to the present day (Jehovah's Witnesses), some have argued that John 1:1c should be translated "the Word was *a* god," because the definite article is missing before *theos*. If so, this would deny the eternality, the full deity, and equality of the Son with the Father. This proposed translation, however, is incorrect for multiple reasons. On this point, see Carson, *John*, 117; Murray J. Harris, *Jesus as God: The New Testament Use of* Theos *in Reference to Jesus* (Grand Rapids, MI: Baker, 1992), 51–71.

6. For a complete treatment of all these texts, see Harris, *Jesus as God*.

Gentile contexts. Second, they carefully predicate "God" to Jesus in order to preserve the relations of persons within the Trinity. Normally, *theos* refers to God the Father, yet because the Son is God, *theos* can also be predicated of Christ. In order to preserve the personal distinctions within God, however, *theos* predominately denotes the Father and *kyrios* the Son. Third, Jesus is God the Son, but he is also human. If *theos* had become a personal name for Christ, it's possible that Christ's humanity could have been downplayed. But with that said, let's not forget that when *theos* is predicated of Christ, it explicitly teaches that he is God.

We now return to the staggering teaching of John 1:14, where we discover that the divine Word-Son became flesh and thus is fully human.[7] But who exactly became flesh? Who is the subject of the incarnation? John is emphatic: it is the Word who became human, *not* the divine nature, nor even the Father or the Spirit. The *acting subject* (what the church later calls "person" [Gk. *hypostasis*]) of the incarnation is the Word. It is *he* who united himself to a human nature ("flesh"), and now *he* subsists in two natures. As God the Son, he remains what he has always been in relation to the Father and the Spirit, fully and equally sharing the divine nature (John 1:1). But now, the Word-Son has assumed a human nature to reveal the divine glory and achieve our redemption. In that human nature, the Son is now able to live and experience a fully human life yet without any change to the Son's deity, since this would preclude him from displaying the fullness of the Father's glory (John 1:14, 18) and accomplishing his mission to save.

This point is reinforced by the concluding sentence of the prologue, which brings us back to its opening verse: "No one

---

7. See Carson, *John*, 117, where he notes how strong John's language is. It's possible that John is responding to an early form of Docetism (Gk. *dokeō*, "to appear"; i.e., Christ only *appeared* to be human). John is emphatic: to deny the genuineness of the incarnation is to deny the Jesus of the Bible and the gospel (see 1 John 1:1–4; 4:1–3).

has ever seen God; the only Son, who is God [Gk. *monogenēs theos*], who is at the Father's side, he has made him known" (John 1:18 ESV mg.). In the Old Testament, some saw visions of God (e.g., Ex. 33–34; Isa. 6), yet they never truly saw God other than in a theophany. But in the incarnate Son, the full disclosure of God is now made visible.[8] John, along with the entirety of Scripture, teaches the exclusive, unique identity of Christ. Who is Jesus? He is God the Son, one with the Father and the Spirit, who now in his incarnation has become human to reveal God and to redeem his people.

Matthew 1:18–25 and Luke 1:26–38

How did the incarnation take place? Matthew and Luke alone record the means by which the incarnation took place, namely, God's triune, sovereign action in and through the virgin Mary. These texts are important for at least two reasons. First, they reveal how the Word became flesh (John 1:14). Second, they remind us that God the Son really became human. The incarnation is not the Son temporarily assuming a human form or taking on some kind of celestial flesh but the Son permanently adding to himself a human nature by the agency of the Spirit through Mary, and in that human nature, he lives and experiences a full human life forevermore (Luke 2:52).

Many today reject the Bible's teaching on the virgin birth, or better, virgin conception, but we do so at great cost. Not only

---

8. A comment needs to be made about the meaning of *monogenēs*. Historically, *monogenēs* (Gk. *monos* + *gennaō*) has been translated "only begotten" (KJV) and used to warrant the Son's "eternal generation" from the Father. Today, many think the etymology of *monogenēs* derives from *monos* + *genos* to mean "unique, only." See Carson, *John*, 111–39. A strong case for "only begotten," however, is made by Charles Lee Irons, "A Lexical Defense of the Johannine 'Only Begotten,'" in *Retrieving Eternal Generation*, ed. Fred Sanders and Scott R. Swain (Grand Rapids, MI: Zondervan, 2017), 98–116. The verdict is still out, but either way, it drives theological reflection on the eternal relation or generation of the Son to the Father, which is demanded by scriptural teaching.

does Scripture teach that it was the means by which the incarnation took place, but also the church affirms it, and theologically, it's one piece with the Bible's entire presentation of Christ as the divine Son, who has become our sinless last Adam (Heb. 4:14–15). In fact, apart from the virgin conception, it's difficult to avoid adoptionism, which teaches that the Son assumes an entire human individual made from a father and a mother who then comes close to or is "adopted" by the Son. In addition, apart from the virgin conception, it's hard to avoid the conclusion that the eternal Son has two fathers—a double paternity—namely, his eternal Father and a biological human father. But Scripture insists that Jesus, as the divine Son, has only one Father; that the incarnation is the Son assuming a human nature (body and soul), not an entire human individual; and that the Son is the subject of both his divine and human natures. Later the church will affirm these truths when it rejects adoptionism and Nestorianism, a point we discuss in subsequent chapters.

When Matthew and Luke are read together, these important truths emerge in two ways. First, the virgin conception is not presented as a strange, weird occurrence in history. Rather, it is part of the fulfillment of God's eternal plan centered on the coming of the promised Messiah. Matthew begins his Gospel with a genealogy (Matt. 1:1–17) that describes Jesus as "the son of David, the son of Abraham" (Matt. 1:1). In fact, the entire genealogy is structured around David, Israel's exile, and now the fulfillment of God's promises in the birth of David's greater Son.[9] Matthew (and Luke), then, set Jesus's conception within God's plan, which creates the expectation that now in Christ, the Creator–covenant God is fulfilling his promises to redeem humanity and restore his

---

9. On this point, see D. A. Carson, *Matthew*, in vol. 8 of *The Expositor's Bible Commentary* (Grand Rapids, MI: Zondervan, 1984), 60–69; R. T. France, *The Gospel of Matthew*, New International Commentary on the New Testament (Grand Rapids, MI: Eerdmans, 2007), 26–33.

creation. The virgin conception, then, is not strange though supernatural; instead, it's the very demonstration that Jesus is both
king and Yahweh—indeed, in a category all by himself.

Second, the virgin conception is presented as the sovereign,
extraordinary act of God's Spirit through Mary. When placed
in the Bible's storyline, the stress on the Spirit's agency conveys
a specific meaning, which underscores the uniqueness of Christ.
For example, anyone steeped in the Old Testament knows that
the language of the Spirit is tied to God's promise of a coming
messiah and the entire messianic age (see Isa. 11; 42; 61; Joel
2:28–32). In fact, in the Prophets, just as one cannot think of
the coming king apart from the Father-Son relationship (2 Sam.
7:14), so one cannot think of the Messiah apart from the Spirit,
thus the Son-Spirit relationship. To speak of the Spirit's agency,
then, reminds us that the child conceived is both God's long-
awaited Messiah and the only one who is able to inaugurate
God's saving reign and new covenant age.

This truth is underscored by the citation of Isaiah 7:14.[10]
The citation reminds us that God's plan is fulfilled in Christ
and that Christ's conception and birth is God himself coming
to be with his people:

> All this took place to fulfill what the Lord had spoken by
> the prophet:
>
> > "Behold, the virgin shall conceive and bear a son,
> >   and they shall call his name Immanuel"
>
> (which means, God with us). (Matt. 1:22–23)

Once again, the child conceived is no normal child.

---

10. Two issues are debated regarding Matthew's use of Isa. 7:14: (1) questions over
the use of "virgin" (Gk. *parthenos*) for the Hebrew *'almah*; (2) how Matthew sees this
prophetic text fulfilled in Jesus. On these issues, see Carson, *Matthew*, 77; J. Alec Motyer,
Isaiah: An Introduction and Commentary, Tyndale Old Testament Commentaries 20
(Downers Grove, IL: InterVarsity Press, 1999), 77–90.

Luke's presentation of the conception is similar to Matthew's but with some added features. In fact, Luke is closest to explaining exactly *how* it happened. The angel Gabriel explains to Mary that "the Holy Spirit will come upon you, and the power of the Most High will overshadow [Gk. *episkiasei*] you; therefore the child to be born will be called holy—the Son of God" (Luke 1:35). This description stresses two points rooted in the Old Testament. First, the virgin conception is set in the context of creation and the coming new creation. Genesis 1:2 presents God's Spirit hovering in divine power over the waters as God begins to create the world. Luke now presents God's Spirit hovering in divine creation power over Mary. What is now taking place is the beginning of the new creation by the Son's assumption of a human nature that the Spirit makes "holy." It's hard to think, as some do, that in the incarnation the Son adds to himself a fallen human nature. Everything in this text speaks about the sovereign work of the Spirit to take from Mary what is fallen, to sanctify it, and to make it "holy"—indeed, "good." The virgin conception of Jesus, then, is not a progressive, natural development; it did not originate in the will of man. Rather, Christ's conception is the divine intrusion of the triune God to bring forth the last Adam, the first man of the new creation, ultimately to undo the work of the first Adam.

Second, Luke's stress on the "overshadowing" work of the Spirit also connects Christ's conception/incarnation to God's unique covenantal presence. In the Septuagint, the Greek verb *episkiazō* translates the Hebrew used for the hovering of the cloud of God's glory-presence under the old covenant (Ex. 40:35; cf. LXX; see Ps. 91:4; cf. 90:4 LXX). Later known as the Shekinah, this glory of God guarded and guided Israel through the wilderness and reappeared in the cloud representing the presence of God in the tabernacle (Ex. 40:34–38) and in the temple (Isa. 6:1–4). Significantly, in response to Israel's idolatry, the Shekinah glory departs from the temple (Ezek. 10) and does not reemerge until the coming of Christ (John 1:14–18), who is the Lord of glory and the fulfillment of the temple (John 2:19–22).[11] Through the virgin conception of Christ, then, God's glory-presence breaks into the world so that this man is truly Immanuel.

Colossians 1:15–20[12]

Another key text for grasping who Jesus is and understanding later Christological debates is Colossians 1:15–20. In the patristic era, this text was used by the Arians to argue that Christ was the "firstborn," that is, the first created being and not God the Son. This interpretation continues today among Jehovah's Witnesses, and sadly, numerous evangelicals are also confused on this point.[13] Against the Arians, however, the Colossians text unambiguously teaches the full deity of the Son and, significantly, that even as the incarnate Son, he continues to do the divine work of providence, inseparably with the Father and the Spirit—a truth that the church's formulation of the *extra* seeks to capture.[14] In chapter 6, we explain the *extra*, but for now let's see how the text teaches these points.

The text is divided into two main stanzas (Col. 1:15–16 and 1:18b–20) with a transitional stanza between the two

---

11. See Paul M. Hoskins, *Jesus as the Fulfillment of the Temple in the Gospel of John*, Paternoster Biblical Monographs (Eugene, OR: Wipf and Stock, 2007).

12. On this text, see Douglas J. Moo, *The Letters to the Colossians and to Philemon*, Pillar New Testament Commentary (Grand Rapids, MI: Eerdmans, 2008); N. T. Wright, *Colossians and Philemon*, Tyndale New Testament Commentaries 12 (Grand Rapids, MI: Eerdmans, 1986).

13. See statement no. 6 of *The State of Theology*, Ligonier, accessed May 7, 2020, https://thestateoftheology.com/.

14. The *extra* affirms that although the Son has assumed a human nature and acts in and through it, he (the Son) continues to act "outside" (Lat. *extra*) it, in and through his divine nature. This entails that as a result of the incarnation, the Son is now able to act through both his divine and human natures.

(1:17–18a). In the first main and transitional stanzas, Jesus is presented as God the Son since he is the true image of God, the agent of creation, and the Sustainer of the universe. In the second main stanza, Jesus is presented as the incarnate Son, who, because of his incarnation and cross work, is our only Redeemer. Jesus, then, is supreme over all because he is our Creator and Redeemer. Let's look further at the text in three steps.

First, the Son's full deity is taught in Colossians 1:15–16 in three staggering affirmations. The Son is first described as "the image of the invisible God," which means that he possesses the very nature of God. The same thought is found in Hebrews 1:3, where Christ is described as "the exact imprint [Gk. *charaktēr*] of his nature." Although different expressions, they both teach that Christ is God the Son. In addition, "image" also suggests an echo back to our creation in God's image. The idea is that the Son is the original image of God *in his full deity* (archetype) and that humans were created to reflect him (ectype). This makes sense of why the Son is not only the pattern of our creation but also the one who becomes human to redeem us, and that in salvation we are patterned after his glorified humanity (Eph. 4:22–24; Col. 3:9–10).

Furthermore, the Son is "the firstborn of all creation" (Col. 1:15). Contrary to the Arian interpretation, the context speaks of "firstborn" in terms of "preeminence" in rank and authority (see Ps. 89:27)—"supreme over." This interpretation is confirmed by Colossians 1:16—"for [Gk. *hoti*, 'because'] in him all things were created" (ESV mg.). The Son is *not* the first created being or part of creation but is its Creator. This truth is further confirmed by the third affirmation. The divine work of creation is attributed to the Father through the Son (hence Trinitarian agency), but also the extent of the Son's supremacy in relation to creation is stated: all things were created "*in* him" and "*through* him and *for* him" (Col. 1:16 ESV mg.). All these affirmations together teach that Jesus is God the Son.

Second, the intervening stanza (Col. 1:17–18a) teaches the same point as it transitions to the work of the incarnate Son. The opening line, "And he is before all things," looks back to 1:15–16. The last line, "And he is the head of the body, the church," introduces a focus on Christ's reconciling work that is developed in 1:18b–20. The middle line, "and in him all things hold together," looks in both directions as it presents Jesus as Lord because of who he has always been as the divine Son and because of what he does now as the incarnate Son. Specifically, 1:17 teaches the Son's preexistence and supremacy over the entire universe as its Creator and providential Lord. In fact, by the use of the perfect tense (Gk. *synestēken*), the emphasis is on the Son's *continuous* providential rule: prior to and after his incarnation. This entails that even as the incarnate Son, Jesus continues to uphold the universe and exercise divine cosmic functions. This seems to require that Jesus is able to act in and through both his divine and human natures, something that the church's affirmation of the *extra* tries to capture. No doubt, this raises some legitimate theological questions—questions central to the debate between classic Christology and various kenotic versions, a point we return to in chapter 7. Here I simply note that in Christological formulation, we must account for all the biblical data, namely, that the Son, even in the incarnation, continues to act as he has always done in relation to the Father and the Spirit.

Third, the second main stanza (1:18b–20) accents Jesus's work as the incarnate Son. The same Creator and providential Lord is also head over his people, the church, because of his cross work for us. Thus, Christ is Lord twice: first, as our Creator and, second, as our Redeemer. But Paul is still not finished.

In Colossians 1:19, he again stresses Jesus's deity: "For in him all the fullness of God was pleased to dwell." This is not a temporary dwelling either (see Col. 2:9). What is true of God the Son prior to the incarnation is true of him postincarnation: the entire fullness of deity (nature and attributes) resides in him.[15]

In this text, as in the entire New Testament, we see the constant emphasis on the Son as fully God and fully human. We also learn that the Son is able to act in and through both natures, without changing either nature. To think of who Jesus is according to Scripture is an exercise in "faith seeking understanding," which the church has done by wrestling with all the biblical data.

Philippians 2:6–11[16]

Philippians 2:6–11 has also been at the center of critical Christological debates. It has served as a proof text for the "kenotic theory," a phrase taken from the Greek verb *kenoō*, "to empty" (Phil. 2:7). In the nineteenth and twentieth centuries, some theologians taught that the Son "gave up" or "emptied" himself of some of his divine attributes in becoming human. In chapter 7, we reject kenoticism for a variety of reasons but first and foremost because this text doesn't teach it—and neither does the

---

15. The truth that the Son possesses all the divine attributes is taught throughout the New Testament. Consider God's moral, or communicable, attributes. Scripture defines God's *love* in relation to the Son (Rom. 8:35–39; Gal. 2:20; 1 John 4:10–12); Jesus is the *righteous* one (Acts 3:14; 7:52; 22:14), even the one whose *wrath* is God's wrath (Rev. 6:16). In terms of *truth*, Jesus is full of grace and truth (John 1:14)—an allusion to Yahweh in Ex. 34—and he is the truth itself (John 14:6). Jesus is the perfect revelation of God (Heb. 1:1–3; cf. John 1:18; 14:8–9). Also, consider God's incommunicable attributes. For example, the Son shares in the Father's eternity (John 1:1; 17:5; Heb. 1:2). The Son possesses omnipotence (Eph. 1:19–20; Col. 2:10), omnipresence (Matt. 18:20; 28:20; Eph. 4:10), immutability (Heb. 1:10–12; 13:8), and omniscience (John 1:48; 2:25; 6:64; 21:17; Acts 1:24; 1 Cor. 4:5; Col. 2:9; Rev. 2:23). No doubt, in regard to omniscience, the biblical authors also affirm, as does Jesus himself, that the Son grew in knowledge and that he does not know certain things (Mark 13:32; Luke 2:52). How one reconciles this tension is part of Christological formulation, but it's important to see that Scripture predicates both of Christ.

16. On this text, see Schreiner, *New Testament Theology*, 323–27.

rest of the Bible. The incarnation is not an act of subtraction; it's an act of addition. In the incarnation, God the Son acts, from the Father and by the Spirit, to add to himself a human nature so that now and forevermore he subsists in two natures without loss of attributes in either nature. Also, it's due to the incarnation that the Son is now able to live a fully human life and achieve our redemption as our new covenant head. Let's look at how this text teaches these truths in five steps.

First, the text is broken into two parts, Philippians 2:6–8 and 2:9–11. In each section, two verbs describe the Son's humbling himself in taking our human nature (i.e., "the state of humiliation") and the Father exalting Christ because of his cross work (i.e., "the state of exaltation"). The movement of the text is from the preexistent Son to his humiliation that results in his exaltation as the Son in a *new* role because of his obedience to the Father. When this text is read alongside other texts, we see evidence for triune agency and inseparable action terminating on the Son. The incarnation, then, is an act of the triune God by which the Father sends the Son, the Son assumes a human nature by the Spirit (Luke 1:26–38), and the entire action terminates on the Son and not the Father or the Spirit (John 1:14; Phil. 2:6–8).

Second, the Son's deity is taught by the phrase "who, though he was in the form of God" (Phil. 2:6). Here is an affirmation of the full deity of the Son with the Father. The text provides a contrast between two forms of existence of the Son: the glory he had from eternity as the divine Son and what he became by taking the "form of a servant" (2:7). The Son who was and remains eternally and fully God has become fully and truly human.

Third, the next phrase is best translated "he did not think equality with God something to be used for his own advantage" (my trans.). The issue is not whether Jesus gains equality with

God or whether he retains it, since the text stresses that the Son shares full "equality with God" (2:6). Instead, the issue is Jesus's *attitude* regarding his divine status. The Son did not take advantage of or exploit his full equality with God to excuse him from the task of becoming our Redeemer. In this way, Jesus becomes an example for us (2:5), while remaining in a category by himself.

Fourth, the controversial phrase in 2:7 "but emptied himself" (or "made himself nothing," NIV) does not mean that in the incarnation the Son subtracted his divine attributes. By the use of two participial phrases ("taking the form of a servant" and "being made in human likeness," NIV), the nature of the "emptying" is clearly explained, namely, the Son's "emptying" was the *addition* of a human nature. Those who affirm the kenotic view make this text say something it does not say.

With that in mind, however, we must not miss the staggering point: the divine Son did humble himself by becoming human and choosing to die on a cross for us (2:8), which is simply breathtaking. In fact, apart from the humbling of the Son in terms of the incarnation and the cross, there is no salvation for us. But this is not the end of the story. Although the glory of the Son in the incarnation and the cross is hidden by his flesh (what is often called *krypsis*), that hiddenness is only our perception of it. God the Son did not become less than God. As he clothed himself in our human nature, he also bore our sins in that very nature. And in that act of obedience, as our last Adam and new covenant representative and substitute, he turned his great moment of vulnerability into the moment of greatest victory over sin, death, and the evil one.

Fifth, Philippians 2:9–11 concludes where this text began, with the Son exalted in the heavens. Only now, every knee will bow and every tongue confess that Christ is Lord in his state of exaltation. In 2:6–8, Christ is the subject of the verbs and participles, but in 2:9, it's the Father who exalts the Son because of his work and obedience. The Father vindicates his Son and exalts him to the highest position and bestows on him the name Lord/Yahweh from Isaiah 45:21–23.[17]

In this magnificent text, Paul captures beautifully who Jesus is and why the incarnation took place. Jesus as God the Son, along with the Father and the Spirit, is Lord of all. To redeem us, however, the divine Son had to become human and die for us. In fact, apart from him becoming the last Adam and obeying for us in his life and death, there is no salvation for us. But as a result of his incarnation and work, the Father has highly exalted his Son so that now Jesus is Lord twice: first, as the divine Son and, second, as the divine Son incarnate.

Hebrews 1:1–4 and 2:5–18[18]

The entire book of Hebrews is centered on Christ and his glory and lordship. Furthermore, in Hebrews, we find exactly what the entire New Testament teaches: Jesus is God the Son (e.g., 1:2–3), who by virtue of his incarnation and work has won our eternal redemption (e.g., 2:5–18). Jesus, then, is fully God and fully human, and both must be affirmed without dilution. God the Son cannot redeem us apart from his incarnation and cross work, but because he became human, God's whole plan and all his promises are fulfilled in him. In Christ alone we are justi-

---

17. This is not the only text that declares "Jesus is Lord/Yahweh." The apostles repeatedly apply various Yahweh texts from the Old Testament to Jesus, thus identifying him as God. For example, see Ex. 3:14 with John 8:58; Isa. 44:6 with Rev. 1:17; Ps. 102:26–27 with Heb. 1:11–12; Joel 2:32 with Rom. 10:12–13, and so on. See David B. Capes, *Old Testament Yahweh Texts in Paul's Christology*, Wissenschaftliche Untersuchungen zum Neuen Testament, 2nd ser., vol. 47 (Tübingen: Mohr Siebeck, 1992).

18. On this text, see Thomas R. Schreiner, *Commentary on Hebrews*, Biblical Theology for Christian Proclamation (Nashville: B&H, 2015), 51–62; Schreiner, *New Testament Theology*, 380–93; William L. Lane, *Hebrews 1–8*, Word Biblical Commentary 47A (Dallas: Word Books, 1991), 10–15.

fied, reconciled, and restored to the purpose of our creation—to know, obey, and love our triune God.

From the opening complex sentence, built around "God . . . has spoken" (1:1–2), the author of Hebrews unfolds the glory of Christ. As the author spans redemptive history, he reminds us that God has spoken in the Prophets but that the ultimate purpose of that revelation reaches its fulfillment in God's Son, our Lord Jesus Christ. In Christ—David's greater Son who is also the Lord—the promised "last days" and God's long-awaited kingdom have arrived.

How does the author warrant such staggering claims? He does so by describing who Jesus is, giving a number of identity statements that remind us of the Son's deity, humanity, and work. He first states that the Son is "appointed the heir of all things" (1:2). This appointment is best understood as referring to the incarnate Son's work that installs him at God's right hand as the messianic king. Yet the author also insists that Jesus is God the Son since he is the agent of creation, the radiance of God's glory, "the exact imprint of his nature," and the Lord of providence (1:2–3). All these latter identity statements are explicit references to the Son's deity. Also, like Colossians 1:15–20, the author reminds us that even postincarnation, the Son remains fully God and continues to act as God, as evidenced in his cosmic functions (Heb. 1:3). The author then returns to Christ's work as the incarnate Son by stressing his work as our great high priest—a work that he did for us and that no mere human (or angel) could ever achieve.

Then in Hebrews 2:5–18, the author finishes his argument that Christ is superior to angels. In doing so, he develops further who Jesus is as the divine Son and what he alone can do for us in his incarnation and cross work. By the Son taking on our humanity, he has become the representative man of Psalm 8—

the last Adam—who as a result is now able to undo the first Adam's failure by his own obedient life and death for us. Literally, in Christ, the promised "world to come," tied to the new creation, is now here.

This text is significant for at least two reasons. First, in a succinct way the author gloriously unpacks the Bible's storyline and explains why God the Son became man. And second, in explaining the why of the incarnation, the author establishes that the kind of Redeemer we need must be fully God and human. He must be human because the only way to restore fallen image-sons is by a greater Adam who obeys for us as our covenant head. Yet he must also be the divine Son; otherwise, there is no full forgiveness of sin.

As we turn in part 2 to the church's Christological formulation defined by the Chalcedonian Definition, it's important to remember that what the church confesses is exactly what the Bible teaches. As the church confessed Christ, especially in light of false teaching about him, the church rightly explained all that Scripture taught, namely, that Jesus is Lord and Savior because he is God the Son incarnate. Later Christological formulation employed a different language to explain who Jesus is, but the language used was not different from what Scripture teaches. Furthermore, the church was extremely careful in her Christological formulation because she knew that what was ultimately at stake was the glory of Christ and our salvation. For Christians, this must never be a minor point. Given who Jesus is, he must be our glory, command our obedience, and receive our complete trust and devotion. There are many good things to be concerned about in our lives but none so central as knowing rightly Jesus Christ our Lord.

PART 2

Theological Formulation

The Establishment of
Christological Orthodoxy

5

The Road to the Chalcedonian Definition of Christ

Scripture teaches us that Christ Jesus is Lord. In the Old Testament, we anticipate his coming. In the Gospels, Jesus is unique in his conception but human like us except without sin. He is born and grows physically, mentally, and spiritually, yet he also knows himself to be the Son of his Father in relation to the Spirit, who shares God's nature and does God's works. From beginning to end, Scripture unveils from shadow to reality that Jesus is God the Son incarnate.

The Bible's presentation of Christ, however, is not the end of Christological reflection; in fact, for the church, it's the beginning. As biblical exegesis leads to biblical theology, it also leads to systematic theology—a "faith seeking understanding." Desiring to be faithful to *all* Scripture, the church has sought to understand "the whole counsel of God" without leaving anything out. For example, given the Creator-creature distinction, how do we make sense of the Creator becoming a human who grows and learns? If Christ is fully God and omniscient, why does he say he doesn't know certain things? Scripture teaches that Jesus was tempted like us, but could he have sinned like us? Such legitimate questions are not always answered in a verse or two; they require careful theological thinking and accounting for all that Scripture teaches.

This is how Christological formulation developed in the church. From her inception, the church confessed Jesus as the divine Son incarnate. But in light of questions from believers, denials from unbelievers, and false ways of putting together the biblical data, it was necessary for the church to exposit, defend, and proclaim the doctrine of Christology. In fact, the first five hundred years of theological reflection in church history centered on Christology in two interrelated areas.

First, the church reflected on Trinitarian formulation. Given Jesus's self-identity as God the Son in relation to the Father and the Spirit, how do we speak of their distinctness from each other and their shared unity as the one God? Are the Son and Spirit equal with the Father (Gk. *homoousios*), or are they of a lesser nature? At the Council of Nicaea (325), the church rejected the heresy of Arianism, a view promoted by Arius (ca. 256–336), an elder in the church at Alexandria, that denied Christ's deity. In the process of condemning Arianism, the church expounded with more precision the doctrine of the Trinity as expressed by the Nicene Creed.[1]

Second, the church, building on Trinitarian doctrine, reflected further on legitimate questions about the incarnation that arose from Scripture. Although the church had rejected

---

1. The Nicene Creed represents the confessions of the first two councils of the church: Nicaea (325) and Constantinople (381). For more on these councils, see Lewis Ayres, *Nicaea and Its Legacy: An Approach to Fourth-Century Trinitarian Theology* (Oxford: Oxford University Press, 2004).

Arianism's denial of Christ's deity, further Christological questions remained. For example, who is the subject of the incarnation? Is it the eternal Son, or is it the uniting of two personal subjects (the Son and a man) to form a composite subject? Was Christ's human nature merely a physical body or a body and a soul? As various false views arose about the incarnation, the church responded with a careful articulation and defense of the biblical Jesus at the Council of Chalcedon (451).

It's important to remember that the church's doctrinal formulations are not equal to Scripture. Yet over the years, the church established orthodoxy in the laboratory of history, testing ideas for their biblical fidelity. Previous doctrinal formulations, especially those enjoying catholic consent, function as guardrails for us today. This is certainly true of the Nicene Creed and Chalcedonian Definition. Precisely because these "rules of faith" faithfully reflect what Scripture teaches, they are authoritative for us as secondary standards. They don't say all that can be said, but given their biblical fidelity, they set the parameters for further reflection, and we ignore them at our peril.

Also, it's vital to note that the Chalcedonian Jesus is not a distortion of the Bible's Jesus. Early heretics often charged the church with departing from Scripture since she employed extrabiblical terminology in her creeds. In the nineteenth century, this charge was famously made by Adolf von Harnack, who claimed that patristic theology was infected by "acute Hellenization." But this charge is false. No doubt, the church used extrabiblical terminology in the creeds such as *Trinity*, *person*, *nature*, *hypostatic union*, and so on. But the church did so in order to communicate correctly the biblical teaching over against various distortions. Additionally, as we discovered in previous chapters, Scripture presents Jesus as God the Son incarnate, just as Nicaea and Chalcedon do, although different language is used.[2] In fact, the truth is that heresy arose when people took Jesus out of the theology, categories, and concepts of Scripture and placed him within Greek philosophical categories. This resulted in views that had difficulty attributing full humanity or deity or both to Christ. These heresies tended to make Jesus a semidivine figure—neither truly God nor truly human—something that the church rightly rejected. Although the Nicene Creed and Chalcedonian Definition employed extrabiblical language, they identified who Jesus is from the Bible's storyline, not from an alien framework. For this reason, the Chalcedonian Definition gives us a Jesus in continuity with Scripture, not in continuity with Greek philosophy.[3]

With these introductory points in place, we may now sketch the basic contours of Christological development in historical theology that established orthodoxy as defined by Chalcedon. The amount of material is vast and complex; indeed, entire volumes have discussed this crucial era in church history that we can only summarize.[4] Yet summarizing the key points is necessary for us to rightly identify and proclaim who Jesus is today. We stand on the shoulders of theological giants who have wrestled with Scripture, have excluded false views of Christ, and have set parameters that help us think correctly about Christ Jesus our Lord.

---

2. On this point, see Richard Bauckham, *Jesus and the God of Israel: "God Crucified" and Other Studies on the New Testament's Christology of Divine Identity* (Grand Rapids, MI: Eerdmans, 2008), 57–58.

3. See Aloys Grillmeier, *Christ in Christian Tradition*, vol. 1, *From the Apostolic Age to Chalcedon (451)*, trans. John Bowden, 2nd ed. (Atlanta: John Knox, 1975), 7–9; David S. Yeago, "The New Testament and the Nicene Dogma: A Contribution to the Recovery of Theological Exegesis," in *The Theological Interpretation of Scripture: Classic and Contemporary Readings*, ed. Stephen E. Fowl (Malden, MA: Blackwell, 1997), 87–102.

4. For example, see Grillmeier, *Apostolic Age to Chalcedon*; Jaroslav Pelikan, *The Emergence of the Catholic Tradition (100–600)*, vol. 1 of *The Christian Tradition: A History of the Development of Doctrine* (Chicago: University of Chicago Press, 1971); Gerald Bray, *God Has Spoken: A History of Christian Theology* (Wheaton, IL: Crossway, 2014); Donald Fairbairn and Ryan M. Reeves, *The Story of Creeds and Confessions: Tracing the Development of the Christian Faith* (Grand Rapids, MI: Baker Academic, 2019).

As we proceed, we will employ the image of a traveled road. Every road leads to a specific destination, and every road establishes parameters within which to travel. Drifting too far to either side of the road leaves the traveler in the ditch. By analogy, the road to Chalcedon leads to the establishment of orthodoxy. Who is Jesus? He is God the Son, who has always subsisted, along with the Father and the Spirit, in the divine nature. But now, for our salvation, the Son has become human and, as a result, now subsists in two natures. As the church formalized this conclusion, she rejected various heresies that couldn't account for Christ's full deity or full humanity or for the subject of both natures being the eternal Son. If any of these key truths are denied or minimized, we no longer confess the Jesus of the Bible, our only Redeemer and Lord. We now turn to the crucial steps that led to Chalcedon, from the second to the fifth century.

The Formulation of Nicene Trinitarian Orthodoxy

To identify Christ rightly according to Scripture, the church first had to think through the relations of Father, Son, and Holy Spirit as the one Creator–covenant God. This resulted in what is known as pro-Nicene Trinitarian orthodoxy as represented by the Councils of Nicaea (325) and Constantinople (381). Two interrelated steps were crucial in this process. First, the church had to create a common theological vocabulary to make sense of the biblical data. Second, the church had to respond to various heresies that denied some teaching of Scripture or failed to account for all the biblical data. Let's look at each of these in turn.

The Nature-Person Distinction

As the church formulated Christology and responded to false views, a crowning achievement of the councils was the development of a common theological vocabulary, especially the nature-person distinction. Scripture teaches that there is only one God. Within God, however, there is a threeness: a distinct Father, Son, and Spirit. To deny God's oneness or threeness or to make the three all the same is to deny the biblical teaching of Christ and to have a false view of God. But how do we conceptualize this? What language do we use to explain Scripture without distorting it?

The church chose to speak of God's oneness by the language of "nature" or "essence" (Gk. *ousia*; Lat. *essentia*) and God's threeness by the language of "person" (Gk. *hypostasis*; Lat. *persona*). But even the widespread adoption of this vocabulary took time since in Greek thought the words *ousia* and *hypostasis* were synonyms; it wasn't until the mid-fourth century that the words were conceptually distinguished by the church. Here is evidence that the church found it necessary to choose language from their culture yet to define it consistently with scriptural teaching.

But what metaphysical content do we ascribe to these words? A "nature" is what a thing is, or, in the words of Herman Bavinck, "that by which a thing is what it is."[5] To speak of God's nature is to describe what God is as the Creator and Lord, distinct from his creation and self-sufficient in terms of his attributes. Historically, theologians have spoken of God's attributes as that which is essential to him, in contrast to that which is accidental. That is, God has his attributes necessarily; he cannot set aside or lose his attributes and still be God. Thus, God's nature is simple, infinite, eternal, immaterial, omnipotent, omniscient, omnipresent, and so on—and necessarily so. Today, some speak of the divine attributes within the thought of *essentialism*.[6] Essentialism

---

5. Herman Bavinck, *Sin and Salvation in Christ*, vol. 3 of *Reformed Dogmatics*, ed. John Bolt, trans. John Vriend (Grand Rapids, MI: Baker Academic, 2006), 306.

6. For a discussion of medieval and Reformation ways of thinking about the divine attributes, see Richard A. Muller, *The Divine Essence and Attributes*, vol. 3 of *Post-*

distinguishes between essential and contingent attributes. Essential attributes are attributes God has by necessity, that is, what he has in every possible world (e.g., infinity, eternality, aseity, simplicity, immutability, immensity, holiness, triunity). Contingent attributes are attributes God has but not in every possible world (e.g., Creator, Redeemer, Sustainer, since God chooses to become these things, tied to his free decision to create, sustain, and redeem). In the past, contingent attributes were viewed more in terms of God's *ad extra* (Lat.), or external, works. Whatever way we think of God's attributes (though I prefer to speak of essential attributes), to discuss God's nature (or the nature of anything) is to describe what a thing is.

What is a "person"? Before we answer, it's important to note that the theological use of "person" in Trinitarian and Christological formulation is not the same as in contemporary usage. Today, when we speak of a person, we speak of an entire individual or of someone's personality traits, or we use it as synonymous with one's soul. But in Trinitarian theology, "person" is not used in these ways. Instead, a person is the who, or the active subject of the nature, not reducible to nature. One cannot separate a person from a nature, but as Bavinck states, a person is "an active subject who *does things* and *to whom things happen*";[7] a person is the subject that acts and lives through a nature.[8] Later, John Calvin, building on others, defined a divine person as a "subsistence in God's essence, which, while related to the others, is distinguishable by an incommunicable quality"[9]—

Reformation Reformed Dogmatics (Grand Rapids, MI: Baker Academic, 2003). For a discussion of essentialism, see Jay Wesley Richards, *The Untamed God: A Philosophical Exploration of Divine Perfection, Simplicity, and Immutability* (Downers Grove, IL: InterVarsity Press, 2003).

7. Bavinck, *Sin and Salvation in Christ*, 306.

8. Boethius's definition is standard: "A person is an individual substance of a rational nature." Cited in Gilles Emery, "The Dignity of Being a Substance: Person, Subsistence, and Nature," *Nova et Vetera* 9, no. 4 (2011): 994.

9. John Calvin, *Institutes of the Christian Religion*, ed. John T. McNeill, trans. Ford Lewis Battles (Philadelphia: Westminster, 1960), 1.13.6.

an incommunicable property that uniquely pertains to the Father, Son, and Spirit.[10]

As the nature-person distinction developed in Trinitarian theology, the church taught that the Father, Son, and Spirit are three divine persons who share equally and fully the one divine nature (*homoousios*, "consubstantial" or "coessential"). In Christology, the church affirmed that Jesus is one person—the divine Son—who, as a result of the incarnation, now subsists in two natures and who is able to live and act through both natures. Although the church assumed some kind of nature-person distinction from the outset, it took time to reach conceptual clarity. In fact, even today, various ongoing Trinitarian debates and forms of kenotic Christology turn on different understandings of this distinction, a point we return to in chapters 6–7.

Trinitarian Orthodoxy versus Various Heresies

As the church wrestled to make sense of God's unity and diversity, a number of false views were rejected, including two views associated with Monarchianism.[11] Monarchianism rightly emphasized God's unity (Gk. *monos*, "one"; *archos*, "ruler, source"), but it denied the coequal deity of the Son (and the Spirit).

One form of Monarchianism excluded Christ's deity by arguing for adoptionism. In this view, Jesus was a mere man, *not* the eternal Son made flesh. Because of Jesus's exemplary moral life, at his baptism Jesus was "deified," or "adopted," to be God's Son by the Logos coming on him and empowering him to

---

10. Since the divine persons share the identical divine nature, they cannot be distinguished by divine attributes. Instead, the divine persons are distinguished by their eternal, incommunicable, internal (Lat. *ad intra*) relations (divine processions): ingenerateness (Father), eternal generation (Son), and eternal procession (Spirit).

11. On Monarchianism, see Harold O. J. Brown, *Heresies: The Image of Christ in the Mirror of Heresy and Orthodoxy from the Apostles to the Present* (Garden City, NY: Doubleday, 1984), 95–103; J. N. D. Kelly, *Early Christian Doctrines*, 5th ed. (London: A&C Black, 1977), 115–23.

do miraculous works. For adoptionism, the Logos is not a distinct person from the Father but is God acting in power on the man Jesus. Because God could not suffer, the Logos departed from Jesus before he died on the cross, hence Jesus's cry of abandonment. This view was propounded by Paul of Samosata (ca. 200–275), and although rejected by the church in the third century, it was taught over a millennium later by Socinians and Unitarians, and today many liberal and postmodern theologians are adoptionistic in their Christology.[12]

Monarchianism also excluded the deity of the Son by denying his personal distinctness from the Father, as represented by modalism (or Sabellianism). Modalism affirmed God's unity, but it denied that the Father, Son, and Spirit are *distinct* persons who fully share the divine nature. Instead, these person-names are only "modes" of the one God who manifests himself differently in history, thus reducing "person" to "nature" and ending up with Unitarianism. One disastrous implication, Harold O. J. Brown observes, is that "the events of redemptive history [become] a kind of charade. Not being a distinct person, the Son cannot really represent us to the Father,"[13] nor accomplish a substitutionary atonement for us.[14] Also, modalism is necessarily docetic; that is, Christ only appeared to be human, unless one argues, which some did, that the Father suffered on the cross (Patripassianism), since the Son is not actually distinct from the Father.

Both these Monarchian views veered off the Christological road into the heretical ditch. They taught God's unity but denied that the distinct Son is God. Jesus was either an empowered

---

12. For example, see the writings of Friedrich Schleiermacher, Albrecht Ritschl, and John A. T. Robinson; see also John Hick, ed., *The Myth of God Incarnate* (Philadelphia: Westminster, 1977).

13. Brown, *Heresies*, 99.

14. On this point, see Brown, *Heresies*, 100.

man or a mere manifestation of God but certainly not God the Son incarnate.

By far the most significant heresy, however, was Arianism, a view taught by Arius, a presbyter in Alexandria, and then promoted by others who argued a similar position.[15] It was condemned at the Councils of Nicaea (325) and Constantinople (381), though its influence continues today, for example, among Jehovah's Witnesses. Yet despite its serious nature, Arianism helped the church define Trinitarian and Christological orthodoxy.

Arianism teaches that God's unity is such that it is impossible for God to share his being with another person.[16] Yet unlike modalism, it affirms the *distinctness* of the Father and Son, but it does so by reducing the Son to a creature. For Arius, only the Father is eternal; thus, the Son had a beginning—"There was a time when the Son was not." Similar to the rest of creation, the Son was "begotten" from God (which for Arius means "created"), yet he was the firstborn in time and the highest of all created beings. Given God's absolute transcendence, God, in order to create, first had to create a spiritual being that could act as a kind of Platonic demiurge (or subordinate god). This is who the Son is. He is God's "wisdom," "image," or "word," but only by grace and participation as a creature, not because he is the divine Son who shares fully the divine nature with the Father and the Spirit.[17]

For Arianism, then, Christ is the perfect creature and our "savior," but he is only qualitatively greater than us. Jesus, as a

---

15. For a discussion of Arius and Arianism, see Ayres, *Nicaea and Its Legacy*; Michel R. Barnes and Daniel H. Williams, eds., *Arianism after Arius: Essays on the Development of the Fourth Century Trinitarian Conflicts* (Edinburgh: T&T Clark, 1994); R. P. C. Hanson, *The Search for the Christian Doctrine of God: The Arian Controversy, 318–381* (Edinburgh: T&T Clark, 1988).

16. See Grillmeier, *Apostolic Age to Chalcedon*, 219–28; Brown, *Heresies*, 104–16.

17. See Grillmeier, *Apostolic Age to Chalcedon*, 227–32.

creature, grows in his commitment to the good and thus serves as an example of how we can attain perfection and partake of divinity as he did. But he is not the divine Son become human, worthy of our trust and able to satisfy God's righteous requirements for us. In truth, Arianism leaves us with a "salvation" accomplished not by God but instead by human achievement. Jesus is simply a creature, an intermediary figure—a god of lesser status than the Father—who is God's agent in creation but mutable, imperfect in his knowledge, and unworthy of our worship. Arianism denies the God and Christ of Scripture and ends up in the ditch. It's no wonder that the church found it necessary to address it head-on, which is what it did at Nicaea.

The Council of Nicaea (325)

The Roman emperor Constantine called 318 bishops to assemble in Nicaea to resolve the growing challenge of Arianism. The Arians presented a statement that denied Christ's deity, but the vast majority of the bishops rejected Arianism, deeming it heretical. The concern of the council was to confess belief in one God, the true Father and his Son, who both share fully the divine nature. Not much was said about the Holy Spirit; that came later at Constantinople (381), where Trinitarian orthodoxy was most fully stated. The Nicene Creed in its 381 edition reads as follows:

> We believe in one God, the Father Almighty, Maker of heaven and earth, and of all things visible and invisible.
>
> And in one Lord Jesus Christ, the only-begotten Son of God, begotten of the Father before all worlds, Light of Light, very God of very God, begotten, not made, being of one substance [Gk. *homoousion*] with the Father; by whom all things were made; who for us men, and for our salvation, came down from heaven, and was incarnate by

the Holy Ghost of the Virgin Mary, and was made man; he was crucified for us under Pontius Pilate, and suffered, and was buried, and the third day he rose again, according to the Scriptures, and ascended into heaven, and sitteth on the right hand of the Father; from thence he shall come again, with glory, to judge the quick and the dead; whose kingdom shall have no end.

And in the Holy Ghost, the Lord and Giver of life, who proceedeth from the Father, who with the Father and the Son together is worshiped and glorified, who spake by the prophets.

And in one holy catholic and apostolic Church; we acknowledge one baptism for the remission of sins; we look for the resurrection of the dead, and the life of the world to come. Amen.[18]

The Nicene Creed not only gives us Trinitarian orthodoxy, but in so doing, it also affirms three key truths that confess the glory, uniqueness, and exclusivity of Christ as God the Son incarnate. First, the most significant teaching of Nicaea is the Son's full deity—something that the church had always confessed but that Arianism rejected. This affirmation is taught in the phrase that the Son is "of one substance [*homoousion*] with the Father." The Son is not merely "from God"; that is true of all creatures. Instead, the Son's nature (*ousia*) is identical with the Father's nature; the Son is "Light of Light, very God of very God."[19]

Second, the creed also affirms the eternal personal distinctness of the Son from the Father. Since the Father, Son, and Spirit share the *same* nature, how are they distinguished? We can't distinguish them by divine attributes because they equally

18. Cited in Philip Schaff, ed., *The Creeds of Christendom*, 6th ed. (Grand Rapids, MI: Baker, 1990), 1:28–29.

19. See Athanasius, *De decritis* 5.19–21, in *Nicene and Post-Nicene Fathers*, 2nd ser., ed. Philip Schaff and Henry Wace (Grand Rapids, MI: Eerdmans, 1991), 4:162–64.

and fully share them. The only way we can distinguish between the divine persons is by their person relations, which the creed teaches by the phrase "begotten of the Father." This phrase refers to the eternal relations between the persons of the Father and Son (also known as the eternal relations of origins or the divine processions) that is reflected in a specific *taxis* (Gk. for "ordering") between them. The Father as Father is "unbegotten," and he eternally and necessarily generates the Son; the Son as Son is always from the Father, and thus not the Father; and the Spirit as Spirit always proceeds from the Father and the Son. Within God (Lat. *ad intra*), then, there are eternal, necessary, and irreversible relations between the persons that distinguish the divine persons and underscore the fully shared deity of the divine persons. Furthermore, as the triune God acts "outside himself" (Lat. *ad extra*) in creation, revelation, and redemption, all three persons act inseparably and as one yet according to their person relations—hence the Father always acts in and through the Son and by the Spirit. As later theologians unpacked Trinitarian agency, they helped make sense of a lot of biblical data regarding the incarnation.

Third, Nicaea rightly locates the reason for the incarnation within God's plan to redeem us. It speaks of the incarnation and the work of Christ "for us and for our salvation," thus reminding us that the soteriological purpose of the incarnation is foundational to identifying Christ correctly. The church was concerned to get Christology right because false views of Jesus ultimately rob us of the kind of Lord and Savior we need.

From the Nicene Creed to the Chalcedonian Definition

After the rejection of Arianism and the establishment of Trinitarian orthodoxy, the church turned its attention to further questions that arose concerning the nature of the incarnation.

As people reflected on the profound truth that "the Word became flesh" (John 1:14), some formulations veered into the
ditch of compromising Christ's humanity (Apollinarianism),
of nullifying the unity of Christ's person (Nestorianism), or of
simply confusing the Creator-creature distinction in the incarnate Son (Monophysitism). In responding to these false ways
of formulating the incarnation, the church gained further conceptual clarity and precision, leading to Chalcedon. Let's look
at each of these views before turning to the theology of the
Chalcedonian Definition.

Apollinarianism

Apollinarianism is the view attributed to Apollinarius (ca. 310–
390), a staunch opponent of Arianism and a good friend of
Athanasius. Given Apollinarius's problematic view of Christ's
human nature, however, Athanasius and the three Cappadocian
theologians (Basil of Caesarea, Gregory of Nyssa, and Gregory
of Nazianzus) later opposed him. His view was rejected by
several church councils but most significantly by the Council
of Constantinople (381).

Apollinarius's view represented a Word-flesh understanding of the incarnation, contra the Word-man view of Chalcedonian orthodoxy. A Word-flesh view insisted that in the
incarnation, the divine Son (Word) *replaced* the human soul
and assumed only human flesh (a human body), which resulted in an incomplete human nature.[20] For Apollinarius, in
Christ there is a substantial union of one heavenly element
(Word) and one earthly element (human body), which results
in one nature—a kind of composite union of the divine Logos

---

20. Technically, Apollinarius was a trichotomist, teaching that humans consist of
three parts: body, soul, and spirit. In the incarnation, the divine Logos displaced the
human spirit (Gk. *nous, pneuma*), thus making it different from ours.

and human flesh forming the self-determining individual we know as Jesus. Yet for Apollinarius, the divine Logos is preeminent, so that in Christ, it's the divine Logos that is directing and energizing the flesh, thus undermining the reality of Jesus's *human* actions, willing, and knowing.[21] As the church later recognized, however, in denying that Christ's human nature included a human soul, Apollinarius had difficulty making sense of how Jesus had a full human psychology, including such things as reason, will, intellect, and emotions. By contrast, a Word-man view argued that in the incarnation, the Son united himself to a complete human nature—body and soul—and thus Jesus had a complete human psychology, including the activity of knowing and willing as a man.

One historical note: Many have identified these views with competing schools of theology in the early church—namely, Word-flesh with Alexandria and Word-man with Antioch—and then have argued that the Chalcedonian Definition is a synthesis of these two schools. For a number of reasons, this historical reconstruction is incorrect.[22] Instead, over time the church came to see that a Word-man view is correct because ultimately a Word-flesh view robs us of the kind of Redeemer we need—one who will render human obedience for us.

In fact, the Apollinarian controversy helped the church to grasp this point. For this reason, the church strongly rejected Apollinarianism on soteriological grounds and with it all Word-flesh views. Christ cannot represent and redeem us if he is not fully human. Gregory of Nazianzus stated this point well: "What is not assumed is not healed."[23] For Christ to serve as

---

21. Grillmeier, *Apostolic Age to Chalcedon*, 333; cf. Brown, *Heresies*, 164.

22. See Aaron Riches, *Ecce Homo: On the Divine Unity of Christ* (Grand Rapids, MI: Eerdmans, 2016), 21–87.

23. Gregory of Nazianzus, "To Cledonius the Priest against Apollinarius," in *Christology of the Later Fathers*, ed. Edward R. Hardy, Library of Christian Classics (Philadelphia: Westminster, 1954), 218.

our representative covenantal head and substitute, he must assume a complete human nature, body and soul; otherwise, our redemption is incomplete. On this point, the church drew a line in the sand: a correct Christology is necessary for soteriology, and for a Redeemer to actually redeem, he must be fully God and fully man.

Nestorianism

Nestorianism is associated with Nestorius (ca. 386–451), the archbishop of Constantinople (428–431), who was condemned at the Council of Ephesus (431).

Nestorianism is identified with a Word-man view of the incarnation, yet it fails to account for the *unity* of Christ's person. Nestorianism insists on the full humanity of Christ, contra Apollinarius. It leaves unexplained, however, Christ's person, how the two natures are unified in him, and whether there is only one subject in Christ, namely, the divine Son. Nestorius's view was that Christ's person is a "union" in external appearance only, a composite of "two personal subjects (the Logos and the man),"[24] which entails that there are *two* persons in Christ.

Donald Fairbairn illustrates Nestorius's view by comparing it to "a firm composed of two partners, one of whom is never actually seen but whose influence is continually felt in all the firm's decisions. The visible partner is analogous to the man Jesus, yet the Logos is the one who stands behind important decisions in the man's life."[25] Words such as "Christ," "Son," and "Lord" "refer to the corporate unity created by the cooperation between the two. The unity is a semantic one because

---

24. Donald Fairbairn, *Grace and Christology in the Early Church*, Oxford Early Christian Studies (Oxford: Oxford University Press, 2003), 21.

25. Fairbairn, *Grace and Christology*, 22–23.

the one name 'Christ' signifies the pair of partners, but the actual personal centre of Christ's being, in this understanding, is the man Jesus himself."[26]

The implications of Nestorianism are serious; it's not surprising that the church rejected it. First, given that there are two persons in Christ, and given that the Word cannot suffer or die, the Word cannot participate in the human events of Christ's life but only stands in the background. This sharp distinction between Christ's deity and humanity leads Nestorius to view Christ's humanity as if it were an independent man or subject, which opens the door to the heresy of adoptionism.[27] But Scripture doesn't teach that Christ's human nature is an independent person acting in relation to the divine Logos. Instead, Scripture teaches that there is a single person, the divine Son, who acts as a unified subject now in two natures, a point that Cyril of Alexandria (ca. 378–444) and Chalcedon affirmed against Nestorius.[28]

Second, in denying that the single person/subject in Christ is the divine Son, Nestorius could not affirm that God the Son died for us in his humanity and thus accomplished our salvation. In Scripture, the human problem of sin before God is a serious one. Our only hope is that God himself acts to redeem by satisfying his own righteous demands against us. Scripture is clear: we don't need a man indwelt by or joined in some kind of union with God the Son to redeem us; what we need is the divine Son to assume our human nature in his own person so that he can represent us and act on our behalf as our new covenant head and substitute.

---

26. Fairbairn, *Grace and Christology*, 23.
27. See Fairbairn, *Grace and Christology*, 44–55.
28. Christ's single person was central in the debate between Cyril, who used *Theotokos* ("God bearer") in reference to Mary, and Nestorius, who used *Christotokos* ("Christ bearer"). See Riches, *Ecce Homo*, 21–87.

Monophysitism

Monophysitism (Gk. *monos*, "one"; *physis*, "nature") is identified with Eutyches (ca. 380–456), a presbyter and leader of a monastery at Constantinople, who was condemned at Chalcedon in 451. Eutyches taught that as a result of the incarnation, Christ's human nature was taken up, absorbed, and merged into the divine nature, so that both natures were changed into one new nature—a nature that now was a kind of divine-human composite.

Eutyches's view was another version of a Word-flesh Christology. As Fred Sanders notes, for Eutyches, the mixing of the two natures "does not produce a third substance equally identifiable as divine and human. Because divinity is infinitely larger than humanity, the result of the Eutychian mixing of natures is not an even compound but a mostly divine Christ."[29] But even though this view is different from Apollinarianism, the result is similar: in this "new" nature, we have an overpowering divinity and a submerged humanity. Later Monophysites insisted that the union of two natures resulted in a *tertium quid* that was neither divine nor human, but the result of every form of Monophysitism is that Christ is neither truly God nor truly man—a view contrary to Scripture that leaves us with a Jesus who cannot redeem.

Christological Orthodoxy: The Chalcedonian Definition

The Chalcedonian Definition is the benchmark of orthodox Christology. It arose out of the Council of Chalcedon, which began in October 451. At that time, 520 bishops gathered to address the ongoing Christological disputes within the church.

---

29. Fred Sanders, "Chalcedonian Categories for the Gospel Narrative," in *Jesus in Trinitarian Perspective: An Introductory Christology*, ed. Fred Sanders and Klaus Issler (Nashville: B&H Academic, 2007), 22.

Only four of the council's bishops were from the West—two from North Africa and two legates of Leo of Rome. Yet Western influence was substantial, owing to Leo's *Tome*—a letter that was written prior to the council and integrated into the definition.[30] As the earlier Nicene Creed established orthodox Trinitarianism, so Chalcedon established the criterion for orthodox Christology. While some have disputed the definition, it has never been set aside. Chalcedon became "the second great high-water mark of early Christian theology: it set an imperishable standard for orthodoxy"[31] as it confessed Jesus as God the Son incarnate in the classic formulation of "one person in two natures."

Chalcedon rejected false views of Christ by rendering a positive view of Christ's identity. It followed Trinitarian theology by distinguishing "person" from "nature." By "person," it insisted that the active subject of the incarnation, "the one and the same Christ," is the Son, who is of the same nature (*homoousios*) with the Father and the Spirit but now has added to himself a complete human nature. As a result, the Son now subsists in two natures—natures that are not confused or changed but retain all their attributes. The Chalcedonian Definition reads as follows:

> In agreement, therefore, with the holy fathers, we all unanimously teach that we should confess that our Lord Jesus Christ is one and the same Son, the same perfect in Godhead and the same perfect in manhood, truly God and truly man, the same of a rational soul and body, consubstantial with the Father in Godhead, and the same consubstantial with us in manhood, like us in all things except sin; begotten from

---

30. See Grillmeier, *Apostolic Age to Chalcedon*, 520–57; Bray, *God Has Spoken*, 350–65.
31. Brown, *Heresies*, 181.

the Father before the ages as regards His Godhead, and in the last days, the same, because of us and because of our salvation begotten from the Virgin Mary, the *Theotokos*, as regards His manhood; one and the same Christ, Son, Lord, only-begotten, made known in two natures without confusion, without change, without division, without separation, the difference of the natures being by no means removed because of the union, but the property of each nature being preserved and coalescing in one *prosopon* and one *hypostasis*—not parted or divided into two *prosopa*, but one and the same Son, only-begotten, divine Word, the Lord Jesus Christ, as the prophets of old and Jesus Christ Himself have taught us about Him and the creed of our fathers has handed down.[32]

As with the Nicene Creed, the Chalcedonian Definition addressed every problem that had so far plagued the church in regard to Christ's identity, and it presented us with a unique Lord and Savior. It sought to curb speculation, to clarify the use of language between East and West, and to function as a definitive statement and road map for all later Christological reflection. Five points sum up the definition, which has established Christological orthodoxy in the church, even up to today.

First, Christ was fully God (contra Arianism) and fully man. Both Christ's deity and humanity are equally stressed in order for him to serve as our Redeemer and to secure salvation for us.

Second, Chalcedon clearly distinguished between "person" (*hypostasis*) and "nature" (*ousia*). "Person" is a principle in its own right, not deducible from "nature" or as a composite element from the union of the two natures.[33] A new person does

---

32. Cited in Kelly, *Early Christian Doctrines*, 339–40.

33. In truth, Chalcedon was still fuzzy on this point, which was later clarified at the Second Council of Constantinople (553). See Aloys Grillmeier, *Christ in Christian Tradition*, vol. 2, *From the Council of Chalcedon (451) to Gregory the Great (590–604)*,

not come into existence when the human nature is assumed, nor does it result in two persons (contra Nestorianism). Instead, Chalcedon affirms that the eternal Son is the person of the incarnation, who has always been in relation to the Father and the Spirit and who shares with them the divine nature. Also, it's a person, not a nature, who becomes flesh (John 1:14). The incarnation is a personal act of the Son (Phil. 2:7). It's the person of the Son who is the acting and suffering subject. Does this imply change in the Son? Not in the sense that the Son changed his identity or ceased to be what he always was. Even as the incarnate Son, he continued to possess all the divine attributes and to perform all his divine functions and prerogatives (Col. 1:17; Heb. 1:3). Nevertheless, in his humanity, the Son lives and experiences life as a human in growth, joys, and pain. As Donald Macleod reminds us, even though God is omniscient, apart from the incarnation his knowledge "falls short of personal experience. That is what the incarnation made possible for God: real, personal experience of being human."[34]

Third, Christ's human nature didn't have a *hypostasis* ("person") of its own (*anhypostasia*). There was no individual "man" Jesus apart from the Son assuming a human nature with a full set of human attributes (contra adoptionism). As a result, the Son, who always possessed the divine nature, now subsisted in two natures as the subject of both. This enabled the Son to live a fully human life through his human nature yet not to be completely circumscribed by it since he subsisted in two natures. This is how Scripture can speak of the Son doing some things qua God and other things qua man, even though it's the same Son who does them.

---

part 2, *The Church of Constantinople in the Sixth Century*, trans. Pauline Allen and John Cawte (Louisville: Westminster John Knox, 1995), 277.

34. Donald Macleod, *The Person of Christ*, Contours of Christian Theology (Downers Grove, IL: InterVarsity Press, 1998), 186.

Whenever we look at the life of Christ and ask, Who said or did this? or, Who died for us? the answer is always the same: God the Son. Why? It's not the divine or human nature that acts and does things; rather, it's the *person* of the Son who acts in and through both natures. It's the *Son* who was born, who was tempted, who died for us, and who rose from the dead. It's the *Son* in whom all God's righteous demands are met so that our salvation is truly of God. As Macleod reminds us,

> In him [the Son], God provides and even becomes the atonement which he demands. In him (in his flesh, within the finitude of his life-time, the finitude of his body and the finitude of his human being) God dealt with our sin. He is a man: yet the man of universal significance, not because his humanity is in any sense infinite but because it is the humanity of God.[35]

Fourth, the union of Christ's two natures in the Son doesn't obscure the integrity of either (contra Monophysitism). Within Christ the Creator-creature distinction is preserved; there is no blend of natures or "transfer/communication of attributes" (*communicatio idiomatum*) that results in a third nature. Yet the two natures aren't merely lying side by side without contact or interaction. Instead, the two natures subsist in the one person who acts fully through both of them but not contrary to either nature. This is why Scripture teaches that the Son simultaneously upholds the universe (Col. 1:17), forgives sin (Mark 2:10), grows in knowledge (Luke 2:52), and dies.

Fifth, the Son assumed a complete human nature comprising a "rational soul and body" (contra Apollinarianism). Chalcedon distinguished "person" from "soul" and located the "soul" within the human nature. The Son, then, did not replace the

---

35. Macleod, *Person of Christ*, 190.

human soul; instead, he assumed a human soul, which entails that Christ had a human will and mind, a truth later formalized in 681 at the Third Council of Constantinople.

In summary, these five points capture the Christ of Chalcedon, who is our glorious and incomparable Lord Jesus Christ. After Chalcedon, further clarification of these points occurred, yet these basic points have established Christological orthodoxy up to our own day.

6

Post-Chalcedonian Clarifications regarding Christ

The Chalcedonian Definition set the basic parameters for properly identifying our Lord Jesus Christ, but it was not the final word. Further reflection and clarification was necessary, which occurred in the later councils held at Constantinople in 553 and 681 and through the influence of leading theologians beyond that time. Specifically, there were four post-Chalcedonian developments that rounded out Christological orthodoxy—all of them consistent with Chalcedon but also an extension of it. Let's look at each of these in turn.

The (En)Hypostatic Union

Chalcedon left us with a number of unanswered questions. For example, given the definition's stress on the integrity of Christ's two natures without change or confusion, must not Christ also have two persons? How do we affirm the integrity of two natures and the unity of the person without veering toward Nestorianism? How can a nature not have a corresponding person or subject?

Also, Chalcedon's teaching that the Son assumed a human nature that was *anhypostatic*—that is, "without a person"—raised a further question. If the Son united himself to a human nature without a human person, then is Christ's humanity complete? How is Jesus like us if his person is the divine Son and not a human person? By the use of *anhypostasia*, Chalcedon could mistakenly leave the impression that there is something lacking in Christ's humanity.

Before we turn to the church's answer to these questions, it's important to remember what the Chalcedonian Definition intended to affirm and deny by its use of *anhypostasia*. Chalcedon did not intend to minimize Christ's full humanity. Quite the contrary: its intent was to affirm that when the Son became human, he did not assume a fully existing individual man, that is, a human person and nature. Instead, the Son assumed a human nature, and he added that human nature to his person. This is why in Christ there is only one person, the Son—thus the rejection of Nestorianism. Chalcedon taught the theological truth that the two natures are not individual agents: natures do not act; only persons act. And in Christ, it's the Son who lives and acts in both natures. By its use of *anhypostasia*, Chalcedon rightly taught that the Son became human not by "adopting" an existing human person but by taking on a new mode of existence as man via a human nature.

Given the negative connotation of the word, however, is there a better way of stating it? By the Second Council at Constantinople (553), *enhypostasia* was the word enlisted, and since then, it has been used by theologians to clarify how Jesus is one person who subsists in two natures.[1] How? It does so by clarifying the concept of *anhypostasia*.[2] Instead of thinking of Christ's human nature "without" (*an-*) a *hypostasis* ([human] "person"), we should think of it as having its person "in" (*en-*) the *hypostasis* of the Son, by whom it is assumed and to whom it is joined. Christ's human nature is not *im*-personal; instead, it's more accurately *in*-personal, since it is individualized as the humanity of God the Son. Thus, the "becoming" of the incarnation does not imply, as Ivor Davidson reminds us, "that God *qua* God indwells or is metamorphosed into a man, but that God the Son subsists personally as a man."[3] No doubt, the Son continues to subsist in the same identical divine nature with the Father and the Spirit, but at the point of conception, the Son becomes the *hypostasis* of his human nature.

What is significant about stating it this way? It explains more precisely how Christ is one person subsisting in two natures. Christ's humanity has no independent existence by itself since it became and now is the humanity of the divine Son. Yet Christ's human nature remains human; it is not mixed or confused with his deity. Also, Christ's human nature is fully human and lacks nothing, yet it's the Son who lives a fully human life, subject to the contingency and vulnerability of human existence. Nevertheless, in all that Christ does for us as our Redeemer and

---

1. Many people have attributed the concept of *enhypostasia* to Leontius of Byzantium (485–543), but it is Leontius of Jerusalem (date unknown, though he wrote in the sixth century) who should receive more credit. On this point, see Aloys Grillmeier, *Christ in Christian Tradition*, vol. 2, *From the Council of Chalcedon (451) to Gregory the Great (590–604)*, part 2, *The Church of Constantinople in the Sixth Century*, trans. Pauline Allen and John Cawte (Louisville: Westminster John Knox, 1995), 271; Demetrios Bathrellos, *The Byzantine Christ: Person, Nature, and Will in the Christology of Saint Maximus the Confessor*, Oxford Early Christian Studies (Oxford: Oxford University Press, 2004), 34–59.

2. For a definition of the words, see Richard A. Muller, *Dictionary of Latin and Greek Theological Terms: Drawn Principally from Protestant Scholastic Theology* (Grand Rapids, MI: Baker, 1985), 35, 103.

3. Ivor Davidson, "Theologizing the Human Jesus: An Ancient (and Modern) Approach to Christology Reassessed," *International Journal of Systematic Theology* 3, no. 2 (2001): 140.

new covenant head, his work is truly a divine-human work because his humanity subsists in the person of the Son who lives and acts for us. As the Son lives a fully human life and renders human obedience for us *as a man*, it's the divine Son who does it. In Christ, then, as David Wells reminds us, "we see all that Adam was intended to be, but never was, all that we are not but which we will become through resurrection" and union with him,[4] yet we also see in him the dawning of the new covenant age and God's kingdom—an age and kingdom that only God can initiate, inaugurate, and accomplish. In Christ, we find our Lord and Redeemer, as well as our sympathetic high priest and elder brother.

The concept of *enhypostasia* was dogmatized at the Second Council of Constantinople (553). Emperor Justinian I called the council to unite the churches and to clarify the Chalcedonian Definition.[5] A series of anathemas stressed the unity of Christ's person and the distinction of the two natures. By issuing these anathemas, the council reaffirmed its rejection of Nestorianism and Monophysitism, provided a needed clarification of Chalcedon, and, as Aloys Grillmeier notes, took Chalcedon to its "logical continuation" as it applied Chalcedonian concepts in a "clearer and more unambiguous" way.[6] After the Second Council of Constantinople, *enhypostasia* became standard in the church. In the East it finds its clearest exposition in John of Damascus, and in the West it was employed by Thomas Aquinas, the Reformers, and the post-Reformation Protestant scholastics.[7] In thinking about the wonder and glory

---

4. David F. Wells, *The Person of Christ: A Biblical and Historical Analysis of the Incarnation* (Westchester, IL: Crossway, 1984), 178.

5. See Grillmeier, *Constantinople in the Sixth Century*, 438–75; Bathrellos, *Byzantine Christ*, 54–56.

6. See Grillmeier, *Constantinople in the Sixth Century*, 456–57.

7. See Dennis M. Ferrara, "Hypostatized in the Logos," *Louvain Studies* 22, no. 4 (1997): 311–27; Davidson, "Theologizing the Human Jesus," 129–53; cf. Geerhardus

of the incarnation, at least four important truths follow from *enhypostasia.*

First, Jesus is personal, as a man, owing to the eternal Son uniting himself to and assuming a human nature. The Son, then, is the sole subject or person in Christ, who gives to the human nature its personal identity without change to his divine nature.

Second, the incarnation is a sovereign act of the triune God that terminates on the Son alone. "The *Word* became flesh" (John 1:14), not the other divine persons, nor the divine nature. Given that the works of the divine persons are inseparable, each person is involved in the incarnation according to their eternal relations of persons within the Trinity, yet it's only the Son who becomes human.

Third, Christ's human nature has everything any other human has in its unfallen condition except independent personal existence apart from the Son. As Herman Bavinck notes, it is the Son "who as subject lived, thought, willed, acted, suffered, died, and so on in and through it [human nature] with all its constituents, capacities, and energies."[8] In fact, it's only due to the Son assuming our human nature in this way that he could become our Redeemer. But this does not entail some kind of vicarious humanity that results in a potential universalism.[9] *Enhypostasia* does not by itself secure the salvation of every human; rather, it secures the reality of the incarnation of God's Son. But how we come to share in Christ's redemptive work is not automatic. It's possible for us to be human and yet not to be "in Christ." The latter is only the result of Christ's entire

---

Vos, *Christology*, vol. 3 of *Reformed Dogmatics*, trans. and ed. Richard B. Gaffin Jr. (Bellingham, WA: Lexham, 2014), 39–57.

8. Herman Bavinck, *Sin and Salvation in Christ*, vol. 3 of *Reformed Dogmatics*, ed. John Bolt, trans. John Vriend (Grand Rapids, MI: Baker Academic, 2006), 307.

9. Contra J. B. Torrance, "The Vicarious Humanity of Christ," in *The Incarnation: Ecumenical Studies in the Nicene-Constantinopolitan Creed, A.D. 381*, ed. Thomas F. Torrance (Edinburgh: Handsel, 1981), 139.

work applied to us by the Spirit, who unites us to Christ by faith and repentance.

Fourth, since the divine Son is the subject of the human nature and is now able to live, think, and act in his human nature (as well as continue to do so in his divine nature), the Son is now able to experience a fully human life (as well as continue to experience the divine life). If we ask the question, Does Jesus possess a human "I"? the answer is no if we mean by "I" a human person. Yet the Son is the one who is the subject of his actions and operations in and through a human body, will, and mind. This entails that the Son in his human nature is able to live, grow, think, and act in a truly human way (Luke 2:52). And in this way, the Son does not modify what a human nature is (it retains its integrity), yet he knows himself as the Son in his humanity by the Spirit in relation to his Father.

Enhypostasia, then, both clarifies Chalcedon and takes us deep into the glory of Christ. To speak of Christ's human nature coming to personal union in the divine Son does not diminish it; rather, it confesses that Jesus is "God in whom our human nature, without its sin, has come to perfect realization, to moral completion, to perfect union."[10]

Communicatio Idiomatum: The Relationship of the Two Natures *in* One Person

Closely tied to *enhypostasia* is the relationship between the two natures of Christ. Chalcedon, contra Monophysitism, affirmed that Christ's two natures were not changed since each nature retained its own attributes—in Christ, the Creator-creature distinction is not violated. What exactly, however, is the relationship between the two natures given their union in the Son?

---

10. Wells, *Person of Christ*, 178.

Some in the early church conceived of the relationship by the concept of *perichoresis*: Christ's divine nature completely permeates his human nature though the natures remain distinct. John of Damascus represents this view when he writes, "He imparts to the flesh His own attributes by way of communication in virtue of the interpenetration [*perichoresis*] of the parts one with another."[11] Some then inferred that Christ in his humanity on earth already possessed complete knowledge, that all the gifts of which a human nature was capable were given him at his incarnation, and that there was really no increase in wisdom during his earthly life.[12] But there are serious problems with this way of thinking.

On the one hand, it seems to undermine Jesus's growth in wisdom and knowledge (Luke 2:52). On the other hand, it views natures as acting subjects, with Christ's divine nature overpowering his human. If not careful, this could undercut the ability of our Lord to render human obedience for us as our covenant head and representative. So instead of *perichoresis*, the church used the language of *communicatio idiomatum* ("the communication of attributes") to speak more precisely of the relationship between the two natures. But what exactly is the nature of this communication?[13]

---

11. John of Damascus, *An Exact Exposition of the Orthodox Faith* 3.3, in *Nicene and Post-Nicene Fathers*, 2nd ser., ed. Philip Schaff and Henry Wace (Grand Rapids, MI: Eerdmans, 1991), 9:46b–48b.

12. See Bavinck, *Sin and Salvation in Christ*, 256–59; Jean Galot, *Who Is the Christ? A Theology of the Incarnation* (Chicago: Franciscan Herald, 1981), 337–57. For how various theologians in the patristic era treated the ignorance of Christ by minimizing Christ's humanity, see Lionel R. Wickham, "The Ignorance of Christ: A Problem for the Ancient Theology," in *Christian Faith and Greek Philosophy in Late Antiquity: Essays in Tribute to George Christopher Stead*, ed. Lionel R. Wickham and Caroline P. Bammel, Supplements to Vigiliae Christianae 19 (Leiden: Brill, 1993), 213–26. For example, Athanasius and Cyril treated Christ's self-ascription of ignorance as "condescension to our human nature," while the Cappadocians interpreted such limitations as related to the economy (223–24).

13. For a helpful summary of *communicatio idiomatum* and the various senses of *communicatio* used in Christology, see Muller, *Dictionary of Latin and Greek Theological Terms*, 72–75; Stephen R. Holmes, "Reformed Varieties of the *Communicatio*

First, *communicatio* teaches that the attributes of each nature are "communicated" not to the natures but to the person of the Son. This is why Scripture can say simultaneously that the Son is eternal, omnipotent, and so on—all attributes of the divine nature—and that the Son is born, weak, embodied, and so on—all attributes of the human nature (e.g., Acts 20:28; 1 Cor. 2:8; 1 John 1:1, 7). How can Scripture say this? What's true of each nature is true of the Son, who is the subject of both.[14]

There are also, however, two other significant conceptions of *communicatio*: *communicatio operationum* ("communication of operations") and *communicatio charismatum* or *gratiarum* ("communication of gifts" or "of graces"). The *communicatio operationum* is crucial in thinking of Christ's work. Owing to the union of the natures in the Son, our Lord's entire work is a divine-human work, and as such, he is able to save us completely. What we need is a Savior who can render human obedience and satisfy God's righteous demands against us. Jesus, as God the Son incarnate, is such a mediator, and it's for this reason that in his life, death, and resurrection, he is all-sufficient, effective, and triumphant as our new covenant head who defeats sin, death, and the evil one.[15]

The *communicatio charismatum* is also crucial in thinking of Christ's work, especially in regard to the Son-Spirit relationship. The church has always wrestled with making sense of the "gifts and graces" exhibited by Christ in his humanity,

---

Idiomatum," in *The Person of Christ*, ed. Stephen R. Holmes and Murray A. Rae (New York: T&T Clark, 2005), 70–86; Vos, *Christology*, 60–74.

14. Classic Christology is not reticent to explain Scripture in terms of Christ's two natures, yet it always predicates what is true of those natures to the person. For example, consider Christ's omnipresence. In the ascension (John 16:28; 17:11; Acts 1:9–11), he ascended and is no longer present until he returns. Yet in his divine nature, the Son is omnipresent (see Matt. 18:20; 28:20; John 14:23). Or consider the Son's eternality. Jesus was only thirty years old, yet he said, "Before Abraham was, I am" (John 8:58; cf. 1:1–2). The former applies to his human nature while the latter applies to him as God the Son.

15. See Vos, *Christology*, 56–64.

especially in his miraculous works. In the early church, some explained this by a kind of "communication of attributes" from Christ's divine nature to his human nature. But as we have noted, this is problematic. A better way of thinking about the "gifts and graces" is Trinitarian, specifically in terms of the Son-Spirit relationship tied to Christ's humanity.

Scripture links the Spirit's work to the incarnate Son very closely. Jesus was not only conceived by the Holy Spirit, he was also given the Spirit "without measure" (John 3:34), thus enabling him, as a man, to live and act in obedience to his Father as our Redeemer. It's the Spirit's unique indwelling, empowering, and anointing work that best make sense of these "graces," so that Jesus, as the last Adam, renders human obedience for us by the Spirit.

In the post-Reformation era, John Owen developed this point well.[16] In thinking through the relationship between Christ's two natures, Owen, following Chalcedon, refused to compromise the integrity of each nature, but he also refused to follow the patristic tendency to account for the "gifts and graces" in Christ by appealing to Christ's divine nature. Instead, he appealed to the work of the Spirit, the same Spirit who shares equally and fully with the Father and Son the divine nature, yet who in his eternal person relation (*ad intra*) is the one who proceeds from the Father and the Son and thus who in his mission (*ad extra*) brings every work to completion. From the divine processions to the divine missions, it is the Spirit who creates and sanctifies Christ's human nature and fills it "with grace according to the measure of its receptivity."[17] Owen clearly stated that these "graces" communicated by the Spirit to Christ's human nature do not transgress the limits of

---

16. John Owen, *The Works of John Owen*, ed. William H. Goold, 16 vols. (London: Banner of Truth, 1965), 3:159–88.

17. Owen, *Works of John Owen*, 3:168.

that nature. The Son, in his human nature, is not infused with omniscience. As Owen commented, Christ's human nature remains completely human, yet the Spirit fills him with light and wisdom "to the utmost capacity of a creature; but it was so, not by being changed into a divine nature or essence, but by the communication of the Spirit unto it without measure."[18] This not only accounts for why the Spirit is the constant companion of the Lord Jesus but also explains how Jesus serves as our true covenant head, representing, obeying, and living by the Spirit so as to secure his work for us.[19]

Here, then, are three ways the church has spoken of the relationship between Christ's two natures united in his person—*communicatio idiomatum*, *communicatio operationum*, and *communicatio charismatum*. In all these ways, we gain greater clarity regarding the nature of the incarnation and how Jesus and Jesus alone meets our every need as our Lord and Savior.

The *Extra*[20]

The third post-Chalcedonian development that establishes Christological orthodoxy is the *extra*. But what is it?[21] The

---

18. Owen, *Works of John Owen*, 1:93.

19. See Michael Horton, *Rediscovering the Holy Spirit: God's Perfecting Presence in Creation, Redemption, and Everyday Life* (Grand Rapids, MI: Zondervan, 2017), 81–104; cf. Dominic Legge, *The Trinitarian Christology of St. Thomas Aquinas* (Oxford: Oxford University Press, 2017), 131–231.

20. The *extra* is often identified with Calvin (*extra Calvinisticum*). As David Willis notes, however, Calvin's *extra* is really *extra catholicum*, given its almost universal status in the church prior to Calvin. It was first called the *extra Calvinisticum* by Lutherans who used it pejoratively in debates over the presence of Christ in the Lord's Supper. Yet what the *extra* affirms is the reality of the divine Son acting in both natures. See E. David Willis, *Calvin's Catholic Christology: The Function of the So-Called* Extra Calvinisticum *in Calvin's Theology*, Studies in Medieval and Reformation Thought 2 (Leiden: Brill, 1966). Also see Paul Helm, *John Calvin's Ideas* (Oxford: Oxford University Press, 2004), 58–92; Andrew M. McGinnis, *The Son of God beyond the Flesh: A Historical and Theological Study of the* Extra Calvinisticum, T&T Clark Studies in Systematic Theology 29 (London: Bloomsbury T&T Clark, 2014).

21. For a discussion of the *extra* in Reformed theology, see Muller, *Dictionary of Latin and Greek Theological Terms*, 111. Muller writes, "The Word is fully united to but

extra is this: in the incarnation, Jesus not only retained his divine attributes, he also continued to exercise them as the Trinitarian Son. Given that the Son always subsisted in the divine nature "before" the incarnation, he continues to live a divine life "outside" (*extra*) his human nature; Christ's human nature does not totally circumscribe the life of the Son. No doubt, from conception, the Son, in his human nature, lived within the limitations of that nature as our covenant head. Yet Scripture teaches that the *incarnate* Son continued to sustain the universe by divine power (e.g., Col. 1:17; Heb. 1:3), which entails that the Son exercised divine attributes "outside" his human nature. Thus, from conception onward, the Son lived his life "totally in the flesh and totally outside the flesh" (Lat. *totus in carne et totus extra carne*).[22]

To make sense of the *extra*, we must link it to other Christological truths we have discussed. For example, the *extra* builds on the truth that the person of the Son is the subject of both natures and acts through both natures (*enhypostasia*). In addition, the *extra* assumes that Christ's two natures retain their integrity and that what is true of the natures is true of the person (*communicatio*). Thus, when the Son assumed a human nature, not only did he continue to share with the Father and the Spirit the divine nature and a divine life, but now he was also able to live and experience a human life. The incarnation did not result in a change in the divine nature and triune agency, hence the texts that teach that the incarnate Son, from the Father and

---

never totally contained within the human nature, and therefore, even in the incarnation is to be conceived of as beyond or outside of (*extra*) the human nature" (111).

22. Oliver Crisp captures two points that distinguish orthodox Christology from nonorthodox in regard to the *extra*. First, in the incarnation the divine Son "retains all his essential divine attributes," and, second, "these divine attributes [are] exercised throughout the period of the incarnation." The *extra*, then, affirms that the Son while incarnate is also "simultaneously providentially sustaining the cosmos." Crisp, *Divinity and Humanity: The Incarnation Reconsidered*, Issues in Current Theology (Cambridge: Cambridge University Press, 2007), 142.

by the Spirit, continued to sustain the universe (Col. 1:15–17; Heb. 1:1–3).

Throughout church history, the *extra* has been consistently affirmed.[23] Cyril of Alexandria is a good example:

> When seen as a babe and wrapped in swaddling clothes, even when still in the bosom of the Virgin who bore him, he [the only begotten Word of God] filled all creation as God, and was enthroned with him who begot him. For the divine cannot be numbered or measured and does not admit of circumscription. So confessing the Word [to be] hypostatically united, we worship one Son and Lord Jesus Christ, neither putting apart and dividing man and God, as joined with each other by a union of dignity and authority—for this would be an empty phrase and no more—nor speaking of the Word of God separately as Christ, and then separately of him who was of a woman as another Christ, but knowing only one Christ, the Word of God the Father with his own flesh.[24]

In Cyril's quote, notice his emphasis on the one person who unites both natures, the immutability of the Son, and the Son's existence "outside" his human nature, so that the Son simultaneously is in the creation and also rules, sustains, and governs that very same creation. This is the *extra*.

The *extra* was also affirmed in the medieval era,[25] although it's often identified with Calvin.[26] But Calvin's affirmation of the

---

23. See Willis, *Calvin's Catholic Christology*, 44–59. For Augustine, see "Letter 137," in *Letters*, vol. 3, *131–164*, vol. 11 of *Writings of St. Augustine*, trans. Wilfrid Parsons, Fathers of the Church, vol. 3 (Washington, DC: Catholic University of America Press, 1953), 20–23.

24. Cited in Willis, *Calvin's Catholic Christology*, 59; see T. H. Bindley, ed., *The Oecumenical Documents of the Faith*, 3rd ed. (London: Methuen, 1925), 214. For Athanasius, see *On the Incarnation of the Word*, in *Christology of the Later Fathers*, ed. Edward R. Hardy, Library of Christian Classics (Philadelphia: Westminster, 1954), 70–71.

25. For Thomas Aquinas, see *Summa Theologica* 3.10.1.2.

26. See John Calvin, *Institutes of the Christian Religion*, ed. John T. McNeill, trans. Ford Lewis Battles (Philadelphia: Westminster, 1960), 2.13.4; 4.17.30.

extra is simply in continuity with what the church always taught. Jesus is God the Son, and thus, in the incarnation, the Son's life and power were never exhausted "by his fleshly accomplishments."[27] The Son's "eternal properties were exercised by Christ during the Incarnation not by the humanity of the One Person but by the divinity of the One Person."[28] Yet the *extra* also protects Christ's full humanity as well. Calvin, for example, argued that the *extra* is indispensable to making sense of the voluntary obedience of the Son as our mediator. What is saving in Christ's teaching, miracles, and death is not simply that they occurred but that they occurred voluntarily. As the last Adam and obedient Son and as our great prophet, priest, and king, Christ fulfills his office as our mediator by undoing the first Adam's work through the whole course of his obedience. The *extra* protects this truth because as our Savior, the Son is able to act as a man without changing the integrity of his human nature.

Given the *extra*, the incarnation is best placed under the heading of *krypsis* and not *kenosis*, that is, veiling versus emptying or losing. Why? The incarnation was the veiling of the Son's deity, not its subtraction or loss. Yet for our salvation, the divine Son chose to subject himself to ignorance, not of necessity, as with us, but in order to redeem us.

In light of the catholic agreement regarding the *extra*, it's distressing how quickly it is dismissed or replaced with something else. The *extra*, however, is necessary to explain how the Son subsisted and acted in both natures. No doubt, explaining the dual activity of the Son is beyond our comprehension. Yet alongside *enhypostasia* and the *communicatio*, the *extra* is a concept required to make sense of all the scriptural data and thus is faithful to orthodox Christology.

---

27. Willis, *Calvin's Catholic Christology*, 76.
28. Willis, *Calvin's Catholic Christology*, 76.

Dyothelitism: The Affirmation of Two Wills in Christ

The fourth post-Chalcedonian development that clarifies catholic Christology is the upholding of two wills in Christ settled at the Third Council of Constantinople (681). Unfortunately, the decisions of the post-Chalcedonian councils are either little known or ignored, especially this one.[29] Yet the council's rejection of Monothelitism (Christ has one will) and its affirmation of Dyothelitism (Christ has two wills, one divine and one human) is important. In fact, it's a consistent application of Chalcedon's two-nature Christology building on the person-nature distinction that helps clarify the nature of the incarnation.

Why did the church think the "will" debate was important? Three reasons may be given. First, two wills are necessary to maintain Christ's full humanity over against Apollinarianism and Monophysitism. Why? Both these false views identified will with person, hence the affirmation of one will, and both continued the problems of Word-flesh Christologies.[30] Also, in locating will in person and not in nature, this meant that Christ's one will is a divine one, thus entailing that Christ's human nature does not have a human will. But as Donald Macleod notes, "For one thing, whatever doubts may attach to the definition of will, it is clear that there can be no true human nature without the ability to make human choices."[31] How are we to conceive of a human nature apart from a human will?

Furthermore, Chalcedon taught that Christ's human nature consisted of a body and a soul, and it did not identify

---

29. For example, John Macquarrie, *Jesus Christ in Modern Thought* (London: SCM, 1990), 166. Within evangelical theology some have embraced one will in Christ (Monothelitism). On this development, see chap. 7.

30. See Bathrellos, *Byzantine Christ*, 89–97; cf. Kallistos Ware, "Christian Theology in the East, 600–1453," in *A History of Christian Doctrine*, ed. Hubert Cunliffe-Jones (Edinburgh: T&T Clark, 1978), 181–225.

31. Donald Macleod, *The Person of Christ*, Contours of Christian Theology (Downers Grove, IL: InterVarsity Press, 1998), 179.

"soul" with "person." Why? Scripture teaches that Jesus had human desires, longings, and aversions. Also, John 6:38— "For I have come down from heaven, not to do my own will but the will of him who sent me"—seems to require a metaphysical distinction between Jesus's will and the Father's will and to require the logical possibility that Jesus's human desires may not always coincide with the Father's wishes.[32] All this demands that in Christ a true human will is at work, epitomized in Gethsemane, where Jesus must choose between two ways and two wills—"Nevertheless, not as I will, but as you will" (Matt. 26:39).

Second, Dyothelitism is decisive for soteriology.[33] To accentuate Gregory of Nazianzus's maxim "What is not assumed is not healed," Jesus cannot be our Redeemer without a human will, let alone serve as "the model for all Christians," since to redeem us as our covenant head, the Son must render human obedience in his life and death.[34] But this is not possible without a human will. Demetrios Bathrellos captures this truth well: "In the Monothelite Christology, Christ's salvific human obedience to the Father is eliminated, and his humanity is relegated to a state of passivity. But such a Christology could not be sustained theologically."[35]

Third, Dyothelitism is required for Trinitarian theology. The will is best located in God's nature, entailing that what is common to all three persons is their divine nature and thus operation, including a shared will. Yet given their personal distinctions, the Father shares and exercises the one divine will

---

32. See Macleod, *Person of Christ*, 179.
33. See Maximus the Confessor, *Disputatio cum Pyrrho*, in *The Disputation with Pyrrhus of Our Father among the Saints, Maximus the Confessor*, trans. Joseph P. Farrell (South Canaan, PA: St. Tikhon's Seminary Press, 1990).
34. T. A. Watts, "Two Wills in Christ? Contemporary Objections Considered in the Light of a Critical Examination of Maximus the Confessor's *Disputation with Pyrrhus*," *WTJ* 71, no. 2 (2009): 467.
35. Bathrellos, *Byzantine Christ*, 98.

as the Father, and the same is true of the Son and Spirit.[36] Yet
if one locates the will in the persons (as Monothelitism does),
the problematic avowal of three wills in God follows, which
runs the serious risk of surrendering the divine unity. Today,
social Trinitarians endorse three wills in God, but they have
a hard time maintaining God's unity, at least in any orthodox
understanding of the unity of the divine nature.[37]

For these reasons, the church officially endorsed Dyothelitism in 681. Numerous people contributed to this decision
but none as important as Maximus the Confessor (580–662).
Although he died in exile prior to the Third Council of Constantinople, his influence was monumental.[38] Maximus made
a crucial distinction between the "faculty of will" (located in
nature) and "concrete acts of willing" (located in the person).
All rational beings have a "faculty of will" and thus the ability
to will. As for Christ, he has the ability to will as a human and
the ability to will as God. Yet it's the person (the Son) who does
"concrete acts of willing." By this distinction, Maximus could
speak of both a person who wills and his will similarly to how
we speak of both a person who thinks and his ability to think,
given his intellect and mind.[39] In Christ, there is one willer (the
Son) who has two wills, hence the ability to will as a human

---

36. See Gilles Emery, *The Trinity: An Introduction to Catholic Doctrine on the Triune God*, trans. Matthew Levering, Thomistic Ressourcement Series 1 (Washington, DC: Catholic University Press, 2011), 83–158.

37. For example, Stephen T. Davis argues that the oneness of the Godhead is not found in the Father, Son, and Spirit sharing the same identical nature; instead, the divine persons are one because "God is like a community." "Perichoretic Monotheism: A Defense of a Social Theory of the Trinity," in *The Trinity: East/West Dialogue*, ed. Melville Y. Stewart, Studies in Philosophy and Religion 24 (Dordrecht: Kluwer Academic, 2003), 42. Also see Thomas R. Thompson and Cornelius Plantinga Jr., "Trinity and Kenosis," in *Exploring Kenotic Christology: The Self-Emptying of God*, ed. C. Stephen Evans (New York: Oxford University Press, 2006), 165–89.

38. For a helpful discussion of Maximus the Confessor, see Edward T. Oakes, *Infinity Dwindled to Infancy: A Catholic and Evangelical Christology* (Grand Rapids, MI: Eerdmans, 2011), 153–60.

39. See Bathrellos, *Byzantine Christ*, 168–72.

and as God.[40] Also, because it's the Son who is the subject of his human nature, it's the Son, in and through his human nature, who wills as a human, thus rendering human obedience.

By carefully thinking through the person-nature distinction, Maximus protected the unity of Christ's person in willing/acting and the distinction of natures and their attributes. Maximus was also able to explain Gethsemane well. There we see Jesus, as the Son, willing and obeying as a human in both petitions. For Maximus, then, "The subject who says 'let this cup pass from me' and the subject who says 'not as I will [but as you will]' are one and the same. . . . [B]oth the desire to avoid death and the submission to the divine will of the Father have to do with the humanity of Christ and his human will."[41]

In fact, only if Christ has a human will can we account for the Son's obedience *as a human*, which is foundational to Christ's work for us. The Son, in his humanity, as Macleod rightly insists, "had ordinary human desires, longings, preferences and aspirations. Just as truly, he had human aversions. Under these influences he made decisions and pursued options in the same way as we do ourselves."[42] In Gethsemane, all this comes to a head; there Jesus does not want this cup and he recoils from it, yet as the obedient Son who loves his Father, he aligns his human will with the will of his Father, as he chooses to act as our representative substitute.

Is the "will" debate important? Yes. Dyothelitism is a necessary entailment of Chalcedonian Christology, just as the other developments discussed in this chapter are necessary to account

---

40. This taxonomy as applied to the Trinity results in three willers (persons) who share the same identical will (nature). The one ability to will as God is actualized by the three persons. Because the one will does not refer to specific acts of willing, we must distinguish between the persons who will/act through the one capacity/ability of will.

41. Bathrellos, *Byzantine Christ*, 147.

42. Macleod, *Person of Christ*, 179.

for the Jesus of the Bible. Ultimately, what is at stake in each of these four extensions of Chalcedon is whether we have a true Word-man Christology that teaches Christ's full deity and full humanity and gives us a Redeemer who can truly redeem, reconcile, and justify us before God by an obedient life and death for us as our covenant representative and substitute.

7

Current Challenges to Christological Orthodoxy

How is Christological orthodoxy challenged today? Broadly speaking, it is challenged in two directions. First, *outside* historic Christianity, the Jesus of the Bible, along with the creeds, is rejected as either implausible or simply false. This is a continuation of what was described in chapter 1, and it requires a full apologetic response as the church seeks to proclaim the glory, exclusivity, and sufficiency of Christ Jesus our Lord.

Within the church, however, and for those who affirm Chalcedon, there is a second challenge. Some accept the creed as a basic "rule of faith" but then revise its theology significantly. This challenge is the concern of this chapter. Today, there is a spectrum of three viewpoints: two revised views known as ontological kenotic Christology (OKC) and functional kenotic Christology (FKC)[1] and the classic view represented by Chalcedon and its later post-Chalcedonian theological developments.

---

1. See Oliver D. Crisp, *Divinity and Humanity: The Incarnation Reconsidered*, Issues in Current Theology (Cambridge: Cambridge University Press, 2007), 118–53.

The mention of "kenotic" Christology recalls a view that originated nearly two centuries ago, first on the Continent and later in the United Kingdom. The theologians who proposed kenotic views were attempting to reformulate classic Christology to meet the challenges of the day and to provide a "middle way" (*via media*) between the "old" orthodoxy and a full embrace of the Enlightenment spirit with its devastating consequences for theology. As with most middle ways, it was rejected by both sides. Orthodox Christians, including later evangelical theologians, rejected the views as lacking biblical and confessional fidelity.[2] Today, however, within evangelical theology broadly considered, although the earlier kenoticism was rejected, there is an unmistakable kenotic influence resulting in a spectrum of viewpoints.

In this chapter, we outline these "newer" formulations. My argument is that neither the ontological nor the functional versions of kenotic Christology are better than the "old" view and that evangelicals today should continue to affirm catholic Christology as biblically and theologically true.

Two Forms of Evangelical Kenoticism

Ontological Kenotic Christology (OKC)

In recent years, some evangelical philosophers and theologians have rehabilited points of nineteenth-century kenoticism.[3] Believing it was dismissed too hastily, they are rethinking Jesus's deity and humanity in kenotic terms. Their aim is to offer "a

---

2. See David F. Wells, *The Person of Christ: A Biblical and Historical Analysis of the Incarnation* (Westchester, IL: Crossway, 1984), 133–39.

3. For example, C. Stephen Evans, ed., *Exploring Kenotic Christology: The Self-Emptying of God* (New York: Oxford University Press, 2006); Stephen T. Davis, Daniel Kendall, and Gerald O'Collins, eds., *The Incarnation: An Interdisciplinary Symposium on the Incarnation of the Son of God* (New York: Oxford University Press, 2002); Ronald J. Feenstra and Cornelius Plantinga Jr., eds., *Trinity, Incarnation, and Atonement: Philosophical and Theological Essays* (Notre Dame, IN: University of Notre Dame Press, 1989).

viable kenotic theory"[4] within the broad parameters of ortho-doxy. Three points capture their overall view.

First, OKC proponents insist that their view is orthodox because they affirm the Trinity, the Son's eternal preexistence, and Christ's deity and humanity. Yet they argue that Chalcedon established only the broad boundaries of orthodoxy. For example, Chalcedon did not define "nature" or "person," and thus, these terms are open to "redefinition."[5]

Second, OKC proposes that in the incarnation the divine Son "laid aside" specific divine attributes, thus choosing to limit himself to a human life while retaining his divine nature.[6] For some, this divestment was temporary, lasting only until Christ's exaltation;[7] for others, it's permanent.[8] To account for this change, OKC must redefine what a divine nature is. Similar to earlier kenoticism, OKC rejects orthodoxy's insistence that all God's attributes are essential to him; no divine attribute can be "set aside" (God's nature is one and simple). For this reason, Chalcedon affirmed that in the incarnation the Son retained all his divine attributes; Jesus was *homoousios* with the Father and the Spirit. The incarnation was an act of addition, not subtraction. By contrast, OKC applies an essential-accidental distinction to God's attributes. In Christ, the Son "sets aside" his accidental attributes but remains "essentially" God.[9]

---

4. C. Stephen Evans, "Introduction: Understanding Jesus the Christ as Human and Divine," in Evans, *Exploring Kenotic Christology*, 5.

5. Evans, "Introduction," 1–2.

6. See C. Stephen Evans, "Kenotic Christology and the Nature of God," in Evans, *Exploring Kenotic Christology*, 196; Stephen T. Davis, "Is Kenosis Orthodox?," in Evans, *Exploring Kenotic Christology*, 113.

7. See Davis, "Is Kenosis Orthodox?," 112–38; Ronald J. Feenstra, "Reconsidering Kenotic Christology," in Feenstra and Plantinga, *Trinity, Incarnation, and Atonement*, 128–51.

8. C. Stephen Evans defends this possibility in "The Self-Emptying of Love: Some Thoughts on Kenotic Christology," in Davis, Kendall, and O'Collins, *The Incarnation*, 263–67; Evans, "Kenotic Christology and the Nature of God," 200–202.

9. See Davis, "Is Kenosis Orthodox?," 115–16. An essential property of x is an attribute that x has and cannot lose without ceasing to be x. An accidental property of x is an attribute that x has but can fail to have and still be x.

By use of the essential-accidental distinction, OKC proponents think they can affirm Christ's "full" deity. The Son freely and temporarily "gives up" his *accidental* attributes (hence Gk. *kenosis*, "emptying"), but he retains all that is *essential* to deity (and remains God).[10] What are the accidental attributes the Son divests? For OKC, that includes any attribute that is inconsistent with a human life—for example, omniscience, omnipotence, and omnipresence.[11]

Third, OKC also redefines what a person is.[12] For OKC, a person is a "distinct center of knowledge, will, love, and action."[13] This entails that within God there are three distinct wills, not one. Christ has only one will (Monothelitism), since the will is located in the person. Also, OKC defines person in relation to soul, so that in humans, the soul of the human nature is identified as the person, and in Christ, the Son (the person) *becomes* the soul of the human body.[14] All these entailments are a serious departure from orthodoxy.

Historically, a person is a subsistent relation, a subject who acts in and through a nature (which includes the capacities of a will and a mind). A person is *not* a soul. Chalcedon taught that the Son (the person) assumed a human nature constituted by a body and a "rational soul" and that the Son subsists and acts in both natures. But given its redefinition of "person," OKC argues that in the incarnation the Son freely assumed a human body and *became* a human soul. While retaining his essential attributes, the Son freely "gave up" accidental divine attributes that are incompatible with human existence and be-

---

10. See Davis, "Is Kenosis Orthodox?," 118.

11. See Evans, "Kenotic Christology and the Nature of God," 190–217.

12. See Thomas R. Thompson and Cornelius Plantinga Jr., "Trinity and Kenosis," in Evans, *Exploring Kenotic Christology*, 165–89.

13. See Cornelius Plantinga Jr., "Social Trinity and Tritheism," in Feenstra and Plantinga, *Trinity, Incarnation, and Atonement*, 22.

14. See Thompson and Plantinga, "Trinity and Kenosis," 170.

came a human person, circumscribed within the bounds of a human body.

Given OKC's redefinition of "nature" and "person," three implications follow. First, OKC rejects the *extra*. In fact, it's metaphysically impossible since kenosis entails that the Son is, at least temporarily, limited by his human body. Second, it entails that God has *three* distinct centers of consciousness, will, and mind,[15] contrary to orthodoxy, which affirms that the divine persons are distinct but share the same capacity of will because they share the same nature. Third, OKC also rejects a staple of Trinitarian theology, namely, the inseparable operations of the divine persons through the one will.[16]

Although OKC affirms that Christ is "one person in two natures," its redefinition of these terms no longer reflects Chalcedon. Yet OKC insists that its approach is "better." Why? OKC proponents think that they view God more relationally (not as immutable or impassible), and thus they believe that they take Christ's humanity more seriously and can discard such difficult ideas as two wills in Christ or the *extra*.[17] Before we evaluate whether this view is "better," let's describe the more common and less radical view of functional kenoticism.

Functional Kenotic Christology (FKC)

There are various nuances to FKC, but the view is best grasped by contrasting it with classic Christology and OKC in four steps.[18]

---

15. On this point, see Thomas H. McCall, *Which Trinity? Whose Monotheism? Philosophical and Systematic Theologians on the Metaphysics of Trinitarian Theology* (Grand Rapids, MI: Eerdmans, 2010), 12–19, 87–105.

16. See Thompson and Plantinga, "Trinity and Kenosis," 189.

17. See Evans, "Introduction," 3, 7–8.

18. Examples of FKC include Gerald F. Hawthorne, *The Presence and the Power: The Significance of the Holy Spirit in the Life and Ministry of Jesus* (repr., Eugene, OR: Wipf and Stock, 2003); Klaus Issler, *Living into the Life of Jesus: The Formation of Christian Character* (Downers Grove, IL: IVP Books, 2012); Garrett J. DeWeese,

First, regarding the "divine nature," FKC insists with orthodoxy against OKC that the essential-accidental distinction is illegitimate. The incarnation is not a subtraction of divine attributes. The incarnate Son is fully God; he possesses the entire divine nature and thus is *homoousios* with the Father and the Spirit.[19]

Second, regarding the "person," FKC agrees with OKC against orthodoxy: a person is a distinct center of knowledge, will, and action. Will and mind are located in the person, not the nature—hence FKC's embrace of Monothelitism.[20] Many also equate person with soul, so that the Son *becomes* the soul of the human body, similar to Apollinarianism.[21] Yet technically, as Oliver Crisp notes, FKC denies that "the Word *replaces an existing human soul*. Instead, the Word becomes the soul of the body of Christ."[22]

Third, regarding the incarnate Son's *exercise* or *functional* use of his divine attributes, FKC differs from classic Christology. Specifically, FKC denies that the incarnate Son continually exercises his divine attributes, such as sustaining the universe and performing miracles. Yet there is a spectrum of thought within FKC about how the incarnate Son uses his divine attributes. Some insist that Jesus *never* exercises them; all his "divine" acts are done by the Spirit, similar to but greater than other Spirit-empowered men. Others think that Jesus *occasionally* uses his divine attributes but that he predominantly lives

"One Person, Two Natures: Two Metaphysical Models of the Incarnation," in *Jesus in Trinitarian Perspective: An Intermediate Christology*, ed. Fred Sanders and Klaus Issler (Nashville: B&H Academic, 2007), 114–53; J. P. Moreland and William Lane Craig, *Philosophical Foundations for a Christian Worldview* (Downers Grove, IL: InterVarsity Press, 2003), 597–614.

19. See Moreland and Craig, *Philosophical Foundations*, 607.

20. DeWeese, "One Person, Two Natures," 144–49; Moreland and Craig, *Philosophical Foundations*, 611–12.

21. DeWeese, "One Person, Two Natures," 147–48; Moreland and Craig, *Philosophical Foundations*, 608–10.

22. Crisp, *Divinity and Humanity*, 50.

his life as a man through whom the Spirit acts.[23] On this point, FKC rejects the *extra*. Classic Christology affirms that the Son lives a fully human life, yet he continues to live a divine life "outside" (*extra*) his human nature since the Son subsists and acts in both natures. But given FKC's view of one divine will and mind in the person, the *extra*, along with texts that teach that the incarnate Son continues to uphold the universe (Col. 1:17; Heb. 1:3), becomes problematic.[24]

Fourth, FKC is often associated with a "Spirit Christology," although the label can be applied to diverse views.[25] Many FKC advocates are indebted to Gerald Hawthorne's *The Presence and the Power*, in which Hawthorne investigates the role of the Spirit in Jesus's life and ministry. He is convinced that the Spirit-Son relationship has been undervalued in theology. Hawthorne insists that the Son, in becoming a man, did not "give up" his divine attributes but "willed to renounce the exercise of his divine powers, attributes, prerogatives, so that he might live fully within those limitations which inhere in being truly human."[26] In this way, Christ's use of his divine attributes becomes "potential or latent, . . . present in Jesus in all their fullness, but no longer in exercise."[27] The result: the incarnate Son chose to live his life totally circumscribed by his human nature (or, in others, mostly so). Thus when Jesus confesses his ignorance, grows in knowledge, or exercises his power, Hawthorne (along with many FKC proponents) insists that Jesus does not use his divine attributes but only acts by the Spirit's power. Thus, all (or

---

23. Hawthorne represents the former view while DeWeese and Issler represent the latter.

24. Affirming the continuing cosmic functions of the incarnate Son distinguishes the classic view from kenoticism. For example, Issler explains Col. 1:17 and Heb. 1:3 by saying that the preincarnate Son decided temporarily to delegate his cosmic functions to the Father and the Spirit. *Living into the Life of Jesus*, 125n31.

25. See Myk Habets, *The Anointed Son: A Trinitarian Spirit Christology*, Princeton Theological Monograph Series 129 (Eugene, OR: Pickwick, 2010).

26. Hawthorne, *The Presence and the Power*, 208.

27. Hawthorne, *The Presence and the Power*, 208.

most) of Jesus's divine actions (miracles) are done by the Spirit, just as with other Spirit-empowered men. Jesus, then, can serve as our example, as he shows us how to live in dependence on the Spirit.

Critical Reflections on Evangelical Kenoticism

What should we make of evangelical kenoticism? Much could be said; I offer three critical reflections with the goal of showing that the classic view is still to be preferred.

Evangelical Kenoticism and the Chalcedonian Definition

Although OKC and FKC claim formal adherence to Chalcedon, they depart at significant points. This is especially so in OKC's redefinition of the divine nature and in both views' redefinition of "person," equation of person with soul, and embrace of Monothelitism. Given these major differences, one must ask, How far can one redefine Chalcedon's theology before it's no longer Chalcedonian? No doubt, confessions are secondary standards and open to revision. Yet given the catholic consensus of Chalcedon, one must demonstrate that the "newer" views are more biblical and theologically superior, which in this case is questionable.

OKC's Redefinition of "Nature" and Its Christological Implications

The most serious objection to OKC is its redefinition of the divine nature and its corresponding inability to uphold the full deity of Christ and an orthodox Trinitarian theology.

First, OKC offers a logical way of speaking of Christ's deity but not a biblical way. Scripture does not allow an irreducible minimum for deity or a divine nature that lacks certain divine attributes. As David Wells says, "The only God of whom Scripture speaks is one who is all-powerful, knows everything, and is everywhere. By definition, a god who has diminished power and knowledge is not the biblical God."[28]

Second, OKC's essential-accidental distinction is arbitrary and inconsistent. As J. P. Moreland and William Lane Craig argue, to say that God has "essential properties like being-omniscient-except-when-kenotically-incarnate, which he never surrenders and which are sufficient for deity," not only is "explanatorily vacuous," but ontologically speaking, "it is not clear that there even are such properties as being-omniscient-except-when-kenotically-incarnate."[29] Also, as Crisp notes, such a view is arbitrary. He writes,

> It is very difficult indeed to know where to draw the line demarcating contingent and essential properties. For if omniscience turns out to be a contingent rather than an essential divine property, then what are we to make of omnipotence, omnipresence, eternity or benevolence, to name four other divine attributes traditionally thought to be essential to the divine nature?[30]

Also, why stop at certain divine attributes? Why not consider the divine attributes of necessity, aseity, and eternality?[31] After all, how can we make sense of Christ's death unless he relinquished these attributes? The fact that OKC does not do so demonstrates something of its arbitrariness.

Third, OKC cannot affirm that the incarnate Son is *homoousios* with the Father and the Spirit if the Father and the Spirit retain all the divine attributes (essential and accidental) and the Son does not. Even if this state is temporary, the

---

28. Wells, *Person of Christ*, 138.
29. Moreland and Craig, *Philosophical Foundations*, 607.
30. Crisp, *Divinity and Humanity*, 132.
31. See Moreland and Craig, *Philosophical Foundations*, 608.

Son does not share the same nature fully with the Father and the Spirit. This not only smacks of a quasi-Arianism, it also, for a period of time, makes the Trinity more binitarian than Trinitarian.[32]

Fourth, OKC undercuts the continuity between the eternal Word (Gk. *Logos asarkos*) and the incarnate Word (Gk. *Logos ensarkos*), thus implying change in the internal triune relations of the persons. For example, in the incarnation the Son "gives up" his omniscience, which means that his knowledge has changed. No doubt, it's not easy to explain the psychology of the incarnate Son. Yet, unlike OKC, classic Christology has the metaphysical resources to preserve Christ's full deity and humanity. The divine Son subsists in two natures—natures that include the capacities of will and mind. This allows us to speak of Christ's real human growth without expunging the Son's eternal divine knowledge. OKC undercuts biblical truth and allows for a change in God.

Fifth, OKC cannot account for the cosmic functions of the incarnate Son (Col. 1:17; Heb. 1:3). Scripture does not teach that the Son temporarily ceased to uphold the universe, leaving the task to be done only by the Father and the Spirit.[33] In fact, Scripture speaks of all three persons acting inseparably and continuously in every *ad extra* work, including providence.

In sum, OKC undercuts Christ's deity and Trinitarian agency and, as such, is inadequate. Nowhere does Scripture distinguish the divine persons by their possession/nonpossession or use/nonuse of the divine attributes. Instead, Scripture teaches that the divine persons equally share the identical divine nature and inseparably act according to their eternal person relations.

32. On this point, see Crisp, *Divinity and Humanity*, 127–31.
33. See Evans, "Kenotic Christology and the Nature of God," 213–14.

Functional Kenoticism's Redefinition of "Person" and Its Christological Implications

Since FKC rejects OKC's view of the divine nature, it's able to uphold Christ's full deity. Yet we must still evaluate whether FKC is a "better" option by thinking through its view of "person" (which is the same as OKC). The problem is that its redefinition of "person" results in serious consequences, and as such, it does not offer a "better" option than classic Christology. Before we look at some of the consequences, let's first outline the different views of "person" at work.

For kenoticism, "person" is defined as a distinct center of knowledge, will, and action. This locates the "act of willing" and the "faculty/capacity of willing," along with the mind, in the person and not the nature.[34] For Trinitarian theology, each divine person has a distinct will and mind, and in Christology, Christ has one divine will and mind (Monothelitism). But how, then, do we account for Jesus growing in knowledge (Luke 2:52) if in Christ there is one divine person, the Son, who has one divine will and mind? OKC proposes that in the incarnation the Son must "give up" specific divine attributes, such as omniscience, because they are inconsistent with being human. Or from the FKC side, the rationale for kenosis is largely due to making sense of how the Son's one divine mind can lack knowledge, given that the capacities of will and mind are located in the person.[35]

The classic view, however, defines a "person" as a "subject" that subsists and acts in a "rational nature."[36] The

---

34. See William Hasker, *Metaphysics and the Tri-Personal God*, Oxford Studies in Analytic Theology (Oxford: Oxford University Press, 2013), 206–7.

35. Hence Moreland and Craig's proposal of two levels of consciousness within the one divine mind and the subliminal nature of the Son's divine knowledge; see Moreland and Craig, *Philosophical Foundations*, 610–12.

36. For example, Boethius defines "person" as "an individual substance [subsistence] of a rational nature." Cited in Gilles Emery, "The Dignity of Being a Substance: Person, Subsistence, and Nature," *Nova et Vetera* 9, no. 4 (2011): 994.

"faculty/capacity of will," along with a mind, is located in the nature. This entails that there is a distinction between the person who acts ("act of willing") and the nature (which includes the "capacity of will"), in which the person subsists and acts. This is why Nicene Trinitarianism affirmed that the Father, the Son, and the Spirit are distinct persons who inseparably act according to their eternal, immanent relations of persons (divine processions), in and through the one divine nature that they equally possess and share. Since the capacity of willing is in the nature, the divine persons act distinctly according to their mode of subsistence *through* the capacities of the divine nature, which includes the same will.

For Christology, the classic view entails that the one person (the Son) is the subject of two natures who acts in and through each nature. Thus, the Son can act as a man according to his distinct human will and live and experience a fully human life. But the Son is not entirely limited by his human nature (hence the *extra*) because he continues to subsist and act through the divine nature according to his eternally ordered (Gk. *taxis*) person relation with the Father and the Spirit.[37] The classic view, then, provides the metaphysical grounding for Christ having two wills and minds. It can account for how the Son can live a fully divine life and continue to act *as God the Son* (as he has always done) and now live a fully human life (through his human nature, composed of a body-soul duality) yet with each nature remaining the same. These explanations, however, are not available to kenoticism, given their redefinition of "person."

So where does this leave us? Classic and kenotic Christology differ on what a person is, and the entailments of each view are significant. How do we decide between them? The answer:

---

37. See Gilles Emery, *The Trinitarian Theology of St. Thomas Aquinas* (Oxford: Oxford University Press, 2007), 51–127, 338–412.

Scripture. We must ask, Which view best accounts for *all* the biblical-theological data, in terms of not only specific texts but also theological entailments? There are at least three significant problems with FKC (which also apply to OKC).

First, FKC has difficulty accounting for how Scripture presents Christ's divine action in his life and ministry. As noted in previous chapters, in the Gospels Jesus's inauguration of the kingdom, his teaching, and his miracles are not merely Spirit-empowered acts; they are also *divine* acts that identify him as the Lord. As the Son, Jesus forgives sin, receives our worship, and exercises divine power. No doubt, these actions are done by the incarnate Son, yet one cannot explain Jesus in terms that merely place him in the category of other Spirit-empowered men. His identity is thoroughly divine; in everything he says and does, he demonstrates that he is God the Son. This truth is especially taught in the incarnate Son's ongoing cosmic functions (Col. 1:17; Heb. 1:3). These texts demand that the Son, even after the incarnation, continues to exercise his divine attributes as the Son, through his divine nature, in relation to the Father and the Spirit.

It's at this precise point, however, that FKC stumbles. Some claim that the Son *never* exercises his divine attributes while on earth; others claim that he *sometimes* does. Either way, FKC, contrary to Scripture, denies that the Son *continually* exercises his divine attributes. In fact, given its view of "person," FKC has a difficult, if not impossible, time affirming the *extra*. But with the rejection of the *extra* and the view of "person" that undergirds it, how does one make sense of the Son acting through both natures and thus continuing to uphold the universe qua his divine nature? The "solution" of FKC—namely, that the Father and the Spirit temporarily uphold the universe[38]—is not only

---

38. Issler, *Living into the Life of Jesus*, 125n31.

denied by Scripture (Col. 1:17; Heb. 1:3), it also surrenders the unity of Trinitarian agency and results in affirming a change in the content of the personal deity of the Son.

Second, FKC introduces further Trinitarian problems. For example, many advocates believe that the role of the Spirit in the life of Christ is the key to making sense of the incarnation. They propose that the incarnate Son either never (e.g., Hawthorne) or rarely (e.g., DeWeese, Issler) exercises his divine attributes. Instead, all or most of Christ's unique actions were done by the Spirit and not him. Yet in such a view, what happens to the agency of the Son in his actions? It's as if the Son disappears and the acting agent is the Spirit alone. This makes sense if the Spirit's agency is the same as in other Spirit-empowered people. In the case of other men (e.g., Moses, Elijah), it's not the man who does the supernatural work but God who works through the man as an instrument. But the case of Christ is different, given that he is the Trinitarian Son. The Spirit is not "external" to him, and the Son, as the subject of both natures, is not removed from the activity of his human nature, even if the Spirit is also acting.[39] In fact, given the hypostatic union, we cannot remove the Son from his own human nature and replace it with the Spirit's "external" action on him. In so doing, Trinitarian agency and order become distorted, and the Son's actions are no longer his.

What is needed is a return to classic Trinitarian orthodoxy, with its definition of "person" and its triune agency that consistently moves from how the divine persons relate *ad intra* (divine processions) to their *ad extra* action (divine missions).[40]

---

39. See Oliver D. Crisp, *Revisioning Christology: Theology in the Reformed Tradition* (Burlington, VT: Ashgate, 2011), 100–107.

40. See Gilles Emery, *Trinity, Church, and the Human Person: Thomistic Essays* (Naples, FL: Sapientia, 2007), 115–53; Lewis Ayres, *Nicaea and Its Legacy: An Approach to Fourth-Century Trinitarian Theology* (Oxford: Oxford University Press, 2004).

This makes better sense of how the Son acts from the Father (John 5:19–30) and by the Spirit (John 3:34; Acts 10:38)—and indeed, how the Son is the acting subject of both natures, the subject from whom the Spirit proceeds according to Trinitarian order and the subject who receives the Spirit in his humanity.[41] In this way, the divine Son alone assumes a human nature, but that nature is simultaneously filled by the Spirit. Christ's humanity receives the Spirit, who proceeds from the Father and the Son. And this reception of the Spirit allows Christ to live and act *as a man* by the Spirit's action on Christ's human nature, so that in his humanity, the divine Son can redeem us as our representative, covenant head, and substitute.[42]

Third, given FKC's redefinition of "person," its proponents undercut what they claim best to preserve, namely, Christ's full humanity like our own. Scripture teaches that Christ's humanity is like ours except with regard to sin (e.g., Rom. 8:3; Heb. 2:14, 17). This truth is vitally important: if Christ is not fully human, he cannot represent us as our mediator. In fact, the kind of Redeemer we need must be fully God and fully human. No doubt, FKC stresses this truth. It also constantly charges classic Christology with docetic tendencies.[43] Yet ironically, it faces serious problems in upholding how Christ's humanity is like ours.

Why? First, kenoticism equates the person with the soul: the Son's assumption of a human nature means that he becomes a human soul.[44] But this entails that the Son did not assume a *distinct* human soul, contrary to the Chalcedonian Definition,

41. See Dominic Legge, *The Trinitarian Christology of St. Thomas Aquinas* (Oxford: Oxford University Press, 2017), 131–231.

42. See Michael Horton, *Rediscovering the Holy Spirit: God's Perfecting Presence in Creation, Redemption, and Everyday Life* (Grand Rapids, MI: Zondervan, 2017), 81–104.

43. See Gordon D. Fee, "The New Testament and Kenosis Christology," in Evans, *Exploring Kenotic Christology*, 25.

44. See Moreland and Craig, *Philosophical Foundations*, 610.

and is thus seemingly unlike us. Second, kenoticism places "the faculties/capacities of will and mind" in the person, thus necessitating one *divine* will and mind in Christ. This means, however, that in Christ there is no distinct human will or mind, also seemingly unlike us. Possibly, one could say that the Son has one will with two aspects to it, but this is not the same as two distinct wills.[45] But if the Son does not act, think, grow in knowledge, and express human emotions as a man (which seems to require a distinct human soul, will, and mind), it's hard to imagine how Jesus is like us and, more significantly, how he can obey for us as our Redeemer.

At this point, kenotic views often assume some kind of "doubleness" in Christ, similar to classic Christology but without its metaphysical grounding. For example, when it comes to consciousness, FKC talks about a divine and human consciousness or a divine subliminal knowledge "underneath" a human conscious knowledge. Moreland and Craig state it this way:

> Even though the Logos possesses all knowledge about the world from quantum mechanics to auto mechanics, there is no reason to think that Jesus of Nazareth would have been able to answer questions about such subjects, so low had he stooped in condescending to take on the human condition.[46]

Or "the Logos allowed only those facets of his person to be part of Christ's waking consciousness which were compatible with typical human experience."[47] This explanation would work if kenotic views held to two wills and minds in Christ. But the problem is that they do not: they argue that there is only one divine mind/soul in Christ. Even more, given their view, how does one divine mind contain different levels of consciousness

---

45. Crisp makes this point in *Divinity and Humanity*, 57–61.
46. Moreland and Craig, *Philosophical Foundations*, 612.
47. Moreland and Craig, *Philosophical Foundations*, 611.

and knowledge? The bottom line is this: a kenotic definition of "person" has a difficult time accounting for how Christ's human nature, at least in terms of knowing, is like ours.

This same problem is also true regarding Christ's will. Kenotic views speak of divine and human willing in Christ, yet their view of person allows for only one divine will. Moreland and Craig argue that Jesus possessed "a typical human consciousness."[48] Jesus had "to struggle against fear, weakness and temptation in order to align his will with that of his heavenly Father."[49] In fact, "the will of the Logos had in virtue of the Incarnation become the will of the man Jesus of Nazareth."[50] The implication of this view is that "in his conscious experience, we see Jesus genuinely tempted, even though he is, in fact, impeccable" (i.e., unable to sin).[51]

On the surface, this seems to assume some kind of "doubleness" for the will. The problem is that in their view, the person of Christ has only one will. How, then, can the divine Son (who has one divine will) make human choices and resist temptation in his humanity with no distinct human will? How does the Son obey as a man? With its affirmation of two wills, classic Christology can make better sense of how the Son is able to live a fully human life and to exercise his will as a man.

Although kenoticism claims it can account for Christ's full humanity better than the classic view, it actually undercuts it. In truth, we are back to what the early church contended for in the famous words of Gregory of Nazianzus: "What is not assumed is not healed." If the Son has not assumed a human nature like ours (a human body and soul), then it's difficult to see how Christ can be our mediator and obey as a man for our

---

48. Moreland and Craig, *Philosophical Foundations*, 611.
49. Moreland and Craig, *Philosophical Foundations*, 611.
50. Moreland and Craig, *Philosophical Foundations*, 611.
51. Moreland and Craig, *Philosophical Foundations*, 612.

salvation. Only if Christ possesses a distinct human will, soul, and mind can he render human obedience to God in our place. We need a Christ whose humanity is like ours except for sin.[52]

Christological formulation is not easy, yet it's our highest calling as Christians. There is nothing greater than to think rightly about our Lord Jesus Christ. Such a task requires the weighing of Scripture alongside historical and theological reflections. There are many pitfalls to avoid.

As the church has done Christology, there has been a consistent formulation, until recent years. No doubt, our theologizing about Christ is never complete, yet one must propose "newer" formulations with great trepidation, especially given the catholic consent on this issue. "Newer" proposals are welcome, but they must always be tested by Scripture and the wisdom of the past. Kenotic views claim to be "better" than the "old" view, but this conclusion is incorrect. The "old" view is still better, and what is needed is for it to be carefully articulated today. In the next chapter, I provide a theological summary of classic Christology by unpacking who Jesus is as God the Son incarnate.

---

52. There are other entailments as well. If the mind is placed in the person and there is no distinct human mind, then how can the Son grow in knowledge? What about Christ's death? If his soul is that of the person of the Son, at death, when his body is placed in the grave, severed from his divine soul, is the hypostatic union undone? By contrast, classic Christology insists that even in Christ's death the incarnation continues since the Son continues to subsist in the divine nature and the human soul. Also, kenoticism's logic seems to imply that the Son assuming a human body brings about permanent limitations and a permanent change in Trinitarian ordering (*taxis*) and action. All these entailments are problematic.

PART 3

Theological Summary

The Orthodox Identity of
Our Lord Jesus Christ

8

Jesus as God the Son Incarnate

We have covered a lot of territory, and the question we have asked and answered in this book is this: Who is Jesus? From Scripture and the church's confessions, the answer is that Jesus of Nazareth is God the Son incarnate. In this chapter, we now need to pull the pieces together. To do so, I unpack ten statements that attempt to capture who Jesus is from Scripture and confessional orthodoxy—truths that Christians need to affirm, articulate, and proclaim today. I group some of these points together to emphasize specific truths, yet all ten are necessary for understanding who the Jesus of the Bible is and how glorious the truth of the incarnation is.

The Divine Son

1. The person or subject of the incarnation is the eternal, divine Son.
2. As the divine Son, the second person of the triune Godhead, he is the exact image, correspondence, and Word of the Father and is thus fully God.

3. As the divine Son, he has always existed in an eternally ordered relation to the Father and the Spirit, which now is gloriously revealed in the incarnation.

Who is Jesus? John, along with the entirety of Scripture, is clear: Jesus is "the Word made flesh" (John 1:14). Yet in stating that it's the *Word* who becomes human, John reminds us of two crucial truths. First, the person or subject of the incarnation is the Word/Son, not the divine nature. Second, the person of the incarnation is eternal, divine, and in an eternally ordered relation with the Father (and the Spirit): he was "with God" (Gk. *pros ton theon*), and "the Word was God" (Gk. *theos ēn ho logos*), thus underscoring the triune relations of persons within God (John 1:1).

Jesus, then, is the divine Son who has eternally shared the one undivided divine nature in relation to the Father and the Spirit, in perfect love and communion, who became a man by the addition of a human nature (Phil. 2:6–8). Jesus, as the Son, is not a created being; instead, the Son is the second person of the triune Godhead, through whom all things were created and are now sustained (Col. 1:15–17; Heb. 1:1–3). It is this Son who is now the incarnate Son, so that by his work he becomes our glorious Redeemer, our Lord, and the head of the new creation.

The biblical evidence for the Son's full deity is abundant, as discussed in chapters 2–4. From the opening pages of the New Testament, Jesus is identified as Yahweh: the one who establishes the divine rule by inaugurating God's kingdom through a new covenant in fulfillment of Old Testament promises—thus doing what only God can do (Isa. 9:6–7; 11:1–10; Jer. 31:31–34; Ezek. 34). Also, along with the Father and the Spirit, the Son fully and equally shares the one divine name and nature (Matt. 28:18–20; John 8:58; Phil. 2:9–11; Col. 2:9). The Son is identified as God (Gk. *theos*, John 1:1, 18; 20:28; Rom. 9:5; Titus 2:13; Heb. 1:8; 2 Pet. 1:1) because he is the exact image and correspondence of the Father (Col. 1:15; Heb. 1:3). As the Son, he inseparably shares with the Father and the Spirit the divine rule, and he receives divine worship (Ps. 110:1; Matt. 1:21; Eph. 1:22; Phil. 2:9–11; Col. 1:15–20; Heb. 1:1–3; Rev. 5:11–12). This is why Jesus has the authority to forgive sin (Mark 2:3–12), to say that all Scripture is fulfilled in him (Matt. 5:17–19; 11:13), and to acknowledge that he is from the Father as the Son but is also equal to the Father as God the Son (Matt. 11:25–27; John 5:16–30; 10:14–30; 14:9–13).

To account for all that Scripture teaches about Jesus and his relation to the Father and the Spirit, the church distinguishes between the person or subject of the incarnation and the nature(s) the person subsists in. The person-nature distinction is a theological distinction necessary to account for Scripture's presentation of the one God who is triune. To explain all the biblical data, the church distinguishes between the Father, Son, and Spirit without separating them into three gods. Instead, Christian theology affirms that there are three distinct divine persons who fully share the one undivided divine nature and that the one simple divine nature wholly subsists in each of the three persons so that each person is fully and equally God.

"Nature" (Gk. *ousia*; Lat. *essentia, substantia*), then, refers to what an object is. A divine nature is what God is in his one undivided essence, which from Scripture and by "reason of analysis,"[1] we describe in terms of God's attributes and perfections. A human nature is what constitutes humanity, namely, a body-soul composite with corresponding capacities, such as a will, a mind, and emotions. "Person" (Gk. *hypostasis*; Lat.

---

1. See Richard A. Muller, *Dictionary of Latin and Greek Theological Terms: Drawn Principally from Protestant Scholastic Theology* (Grand Rapids, MI: Baker, 1985), 94.

persona, *subsistentia*), however, is the subject of the nature, and it subsists in a nature and acts through it. Persons are "acting subjects"; natures are not. In the incarnation, then, the Son (the person), who subsists eternally in the one divine nature with the Father and the Spirit, acted to assume a human nature (John 1:14; Phil. 2:6–8) and now is able to act through both natures.

Scripture requires that a person-nature distinction be made, but not everyone agrees on the content of each concept. In fact, crucial differences in Christological formulations are due to differences regarding this distinction, a point discussed in chapter 7 regarding kenoticism. Today, many define a person as a "distinct center of knowledge, will, love, and action,"[2] but, as noted, this view creates more problems than it solves. Given the importance of this distinction for theology, it's necessary to reflect further on it: to explain the classic view of person and then to apply it to Trinitarian relations and Christology.

A Classic View of "Person"

A person is (1) ontologically distinct from nature; (2) the subject or "I" of a nature, with a nature consisting of a thing's attributes and capacities (e.g., will, mind); and (3) not a soul.

Probably the most influential definition of "person" is from Boethius: "an individual substance of a rational nature."[3] As developed over time, "individual substance" was understood as a "subject" or "I" subsisting in a nature,[4] who acts through a "rational nature" (which includes the capacities of will, mind, etc.). As applied to Christology, a *human* "rational nature" is

---

2. See William Hasker, *Metaphysics and the Tri-Personal God*, Oxford Studies in Analytic Theology (Oxford: Oxford University Press, 2013), 19–25.

3. Cited in Gilles Emery, "The Dignity of Being a Substance: Person, Subsistence, and Nature," *Nova et Vetera* 9, no. 4 (2011): 994.

4. Emery, "Dignity of Being a Substance," 995.

the body-soul composite that the Son assumes, and by this assumption, the Son (person) is fully human and able to act in and through it.[5]

In defining "person," however, we must also distinguish between divine and human persons. Given the Creator-creature distinction, divine persons are the archetype to the human ectype, and the relationship between them is not univocal but analogical. Divine and human persons are similar but never the same. So what is a divine person?

To build on our initial definition of person, a divine person is a "subsisting relation"[6] in the one indivisible divine nature, unlike human persons, who subsist only in their own nature. But if the divine nature completely subsists in each person, how are the divine persons distinct? The persons are not distinguished by divine attributes since each person shares the divine nature fully and completely. Instead, the persons are distinguished by their eternal, immanent (*ad intra*) person relations known by revelation, owing to God's actions in creation and redemption (*ad extra*). Or, to state it another way, the divine persons are distinguished by their own personal "mode of subsisting" in the divine nature that is different from and "incommunicable"[7] to the other persons (i.e., the divine processions). So the Father is distinguished by the relation of paternity; the Son by filiation, or eternal generation, from the Father; and the Spirit by spiration, or eternal procession, from

---

5. On the person-nature distinction and the relationship between them, see Herman Bavinck, *Sin and Salvation in Christ*, vol. 3 of *Reformed Dogmatics*, ed. John Bolt, trans. John Vriend (Grand Rapids, MI: Baker Academic, 2006), 306. He writes that a person is "the owner, possessor, and master of a nature, a completion of existence, sustaining and determining the existence of a nature, the subject that lives, thinks, wills, and acts through nature with all its abundant content, by which nature becomes self-existent and is not an accident of another entity."

6. Thomas Aquinas, *Summa Theologica* (repr., Notre Dame, IN: Christian Classics, 1981), 1:205 (40.2.1).

7. John Calvin, *Institutes of the Christian Religion*, ed. John T. McNeill, trans. Ford Lewis Battles (Philadelphia: Westminster, 1960), 1.13.6.

the Father and the Son. Each divine person is God, possessing all that is the divine nature yet distinguished by their personal mode of subsistence.[8]

Human persons, on the other hand, are not subsisting relations in the same nature. Rather, each human person is finite, subsisting in its concrete nature. No human person subsists in more than its own nature, and no human person shares the same nature with another human person. Individual humans are identified by the principle of subsisting (i.e., the person or the subject of the nature) and the principle of distinction (i.e., a concrete human nature). All concrete human natures are the same kind of nature but not the same instance of it. Yet a human person is analogous to divine persons because it subsists in and acts through a nature.[9] In Christ, there is enough similarity since when the divine Son assumes a human nature without a human person (*anhypostasia*, contra Nestorianism), he is able to "personalize" (*enhypostasia*) his human nature and be fully human although his person is the divine Son.

Why is this discussion important for Christology and understanding the incarnation? A proper comprehension of the person-nature distinction is crucial in making rational sense of the biblical presentation that Jesus is God the Son incarnate. The divine person (the Son) subsisting in the divine nature did not become a human person but assumed a human nature so that the same Son is the subject who continues to subsist in the divine nature as God and now in a human nature as a man. Through the divine nature, the Son continues to act as God. And through his human nature, the eternal Son "asserts itself within a human consciousness and in human language. It is the divine 'I' of a

8. See Emery, "Dignity of Being a Substance," 997–1001; cf. Gilles Emery, *The Trinitarian Theology of St. Thomas Aquinas* (Oxford: Oxford University Press, 2007), 51–150.

9. See Emery, "Dignity of Being a Substance," 997–1001.

man who is living a genuinely human life."[10] This is why Jesus can stand face-to-face with the Jewish leaders and declare that he is God: "Truly, truly, I say to you, before Abraham was, I am" (John 8:58). He can do so because the divine Son, the second person of the triune Godhead, is the one who says it. It is he, as the Son, who has assumed a human nature, and it is he who speaks through human vocal cords and declares that he is God.

The Triune Persons and Their Relations

To think rightly about the incarnation, we must also reflect on the Son's relation to the Father and the Spirit. God as triune grounds Christology; apart from understanding the eternal relations of the divine persons, we cannot make sense of who Jesus is. Herman Bavinck rightly speaks of the organic relationship between God's triune existence and the Son's incarnation: "The incarnation has its presupposition and foundation in the trinitarian being of God. In Deism and pantheism there is no room for an incarnation of God."[11] In fact, thinking through the triune relations of the persons will allow us to theologize further about the incarnation and specifically answer three questions: Why did the Son alone become incarnate? How does the incarnate Son relate to the Father? How does the incarnate Son relate to the Spirit?

To answer these questions, let's first reflect on the relations between the triune persons. Through divine revelation and God's actions in history, we learn how the divine persons have eternally and necessarily related to each other according to their personal "mode of subsistence" in the divine nature. Although God has not given us an exhaustive revelation of himself, we

---

10. Jean Galot, *Who Is Christ? A Theology of the Incarnation* (Chicago: Franciscan Herald, 1981), 322.

11. Bavinck, *Sin and Salvation in Christ*, 274.

expect a continuity between the *ad intra* person relations (the divine processions) and God's *ad extra* actions (the divine missions) as they function in redemptive history (or the economy).

As noted, the Father, Son, and Spirit are distinguished by their eternal, immanent relations of persons, which result in a specific "ordering" (Gk. *taxis*), and that ordering is disclosed in God's *ad extra* actions, including the incarnation.[12] The Father is first, has paternity because of his relation to the Son, and is the one who initiates and sends. The Son has filiation and is eternally generated from the Father. The Spirit has spiration and eternally proceeds from the Father and the Son. In God's acts, all three persons inseparably act through the one divine nature. Yet each person acts distinctly, with specific actions terminating on persons according to their eternally ordered relations of persons, or mode of subsistence, in the divine nature. The result: every external act of God is one and undivided (Lat. *opera Trinitatis ad extra sunt indivisa*), yet the Father initiates and acts through the Son, the Son acts from the Father, and the Spirit acts from the Father and the Son. With this basic Trinitarian theology in place, we may now return to the three questions and discover how God's triune relations are displayed in the incarnation.

First, why did the Son alone become incarnate? What eternally and necessarily distinguishes the Son is that he is the Son of the Father, who as the Son, Word, and image is the perfect revelation of the Father, the one through whom the Father acts, and the archetype of our human creation as God's image. As such, it is fitting that he alone become human. By assuming and acting through a created human nature, the Son redeems, restores, and glorifies his people so that we are restored to our

---

12. See Gilles Emery, *Trinity, Church, and the Human Person: Thomistic Essays* (Naples, FL: Sapientia, 2007), 115–53.

creaturely image bearing and sonship. Thus, given who the Son is in relation to the Father and the Spirit, it is fitting that he become the incarnate, obedient Son and do the will of the Father, as he has always done but now does as a man by the Spirit.[13] In this way, the incarnation is the outworking of who the triune God is. Scott Swain captures this point well:

> The story of Jesus, as it unfolds in his filial relationship to his Father in the power of the Spirit, is simply *the being of the triune God in the temporal, self-manifesting, self-communicating execution of his eternal resolve to become our God.*[14]

Second, how does the incarnate Son relate to his Father? The incarnate Son relates to his Father in divine-filial relation as he has from eternity but now also in willing obedience to his Father's will for our salvation. In fact, because of the incarnation, the Son is able to live and act through both natures, yet his action is always from the Father and by the Spirit. As the Son of the Father, he is the one through whom the Father created all things, and he is the one who continues to sustain and govern all things even in his incarnation. Yet the same Son has never acted independently of the Father, and as the Son, in his humanity, he continues to live in total dependence on the Father but now within the limits of his human nature: "Jesus depends upon the Father for his life ([John] 5:16), power (5:19), knowledge (8:16), message (7:16), mission (7:28), instruction (14:31), authority (17:2), glory (17:24) and love (10:17)."[15]

---

13. See Dominic Legge, *The Trinitarian Christology of St. Thomas Aquinas* (Oxford: Oxford University Press, 2017), 61–102.

14. Scott R. Swain, *The God of the Gospel: Robert Jenson's Trinitarian Theology*, Strategic Initiatives in Evangelical Theology (Downers Grove, IL: IVP Academic, 2013), 190; emphasis original.

15. Andreas J. Köstenberger and Scott R. Swain, *Father, Son and Spirit: The Trinity in John's Gospel*, New Studies in Biblical Theology 24 (Downers Grove, IL: InterVarsity Press, 2008), 118.

As the Son, he could do only what he saw his Father doing (John 5:19); as the incarnate Son, Jesus was a man under the Father's authority. Yet his relation to his Father was not new; the Son was always from the Father. Given this divine-filial relation, texts such as John 14:28 (cf. 1 Cor. 15:27–28) make sense because they speak of the personal priority of the Father. The Father is first in the *taxis* ("ordering") of the triune life, not ontologically superior. The Father is the "source of the Godhead" (Lat. *fons divinitatis*) in the divine processions, not in having more deity. All three persons are fully God, yet they are distinguished according to their ordered person relations.

In fact, the incarnate Son's obedience is not a violation of his deity but the truest expression of his eternal filial relation to the Father: "The Son's obedience to the Father's charge does not compromise the Son's authority to act but rather establishes it. He is the free Lord of all—including his own death—*as* the Son who obeys the Father."[16]

Third, how does the incarnate Son relate to the Spirit? The incarnate Son relates to the other divine persons as he has from eternity: from the Father and by the Spirit. But now he also relates to them in light of the incarnation and his saving work. In the incarnation, God acts as one, yet only the Son assumes a human nature and becomes present in that nature in a new mode of existing. Still, he has done so from the Father and by the Spirit, and as the Son, he has also sent the Spirit and received the Spirit in his human nature. Dominic Legge captures this truth well:

> When the Word is personally united to the human nature of Christ, that Word breathes forth or bursts into Love—that is, the Word bestows the Holy Spirit on that human nature

---

16. Köstenberger and Swain, *Father, Son and Spirit*, 122; emphasis original.

in the gift of habitual grace, which blossoms in wisdom and love, so that Christ knows and loves God perfectly in that nature and according to a properly human mode. . . . Christ's human nature is hypostatically united to the Son alone, but it is simultaneously filled with the presence of the Holy Spirit because the Son and the Spirit are never apart: the Holy Spirit is the Son's own Spirit. God acts in the economy of grace as he is in himself—as a Trinity of persons in which the Spirit proceeds from the Son.[17]

The triune relations, specifically the Son-Spirit relation, best explain the "gifts and graces" displayed by the incarnate Son. From conception on, the Spirit acts on and sanctifies Christ's human nature. In fact, Jesus is given the Spirit without measure (John 3:34), which explains how he lives his life as the last Adam (Rom. 5:18–21; Heb. 2:5–18) for us and secures our redemption (Luke 1:35; 2:52; John 3:34; Acts 10:38). By the Spirit, the Son in his humanity is gifted, indwelt, and empowered to carry out his work for us. By the Spirit, he learns obedience, thus perfectly qualifying him to represent us as our new covenant head and to die for us as our penal substitute (Heb. 5:8–10; cf. Rom. 3:21–26). By the Spirit, he is raised and glorified, becoming the first man of the new creation and the pattern of our glorification (1 Cor. 15:45–49).

It is also important to note, however, that although the "graces" communicated to Christ's human nature did not transgress the limits of that nature and make it superhuman, Christ's possession of the Spirit was greater than any previous Spirit-empowered man. Jesus had the Spirit without measure, and his human nature was gifted and empowered to the fullest extent. As the Son, he was eternally related to the Spirit, and even in

17. Legge, *Trinitarian Christology*, 152–53.

his humanity, the Son experienced and possessed the Spirit fully and continuously "according to the full capacity of a human nature for union with God."[18] This included a fullness of revelatory knowledge, yet proportionate to his human mind and a gifting of the Spirit, so that the Son acted and willed as a man in perfect love and obedience to his Father's will by the Spirit (Matt. 26:36–42; John 10:14–18; Heb. 10:5–10).

These initial three truths teach us that to know who Jesus is, we must first grasp that the person of the incarnation is the Trinitarian Son. And to think properly about him, we must think in terms of eternal triune relations; otherwise, we will never comprehend the truth that it is this Son who became flesh (John 1:1, 14) to redeem his people from their sins (Matt. 1:21).

The Incarnation

4. The incarnation is an act of addition, not subtraction.
5. The virgin conception was the glorious means by which the incarnation took place.
6. The human nature assumed by the divine Son is fully human, unfallen, and sinless.

The next three statements focus on the nature of the incarnation, namely, how "the Word became flesh" (John 1:14) and what happened when he did. From eternity, the Son, in relation to the Father and the Spirit, subsisted in the divine nature. Now, as a result of the incarnation, the Son, without change or loss of his deity, added a second nature, namely, a human nature consisting of a human body and soul (Phil. 2:6–8). As a result, the Son added a human dimension to his personal divine life and became present to us in a new mode of existence as the incarnate Son. Yet the Son's subsistence and action in both

---

18. Legge, *Trinitarian Christology*, 168.

natures is consistent with the integrity of both, without either nature ever being mutually exclusive of the other. Given the incarnation, the Son is able to act by his two natures and produce effects proper to each nature and thus accomplish our salvation as the divine Son who obeys for us in his life and death as our covenant representative and substitute.

How did the incarnation occur? It happened by the virgin conception, which was the sovereign, effectual means by which the Son assumed a human nature (Matt. 1:18–25; Luke 1:26–38). The act was triune: the Father sent the Son, the incarnation terminated on the Son, and the Spirit acted on Mary to sanctify her contribution and create a human nature for the Son. The incarnation was thoroughly supernatural, the fulfillment of Old Testament expectations, and a glorious demonstration of God's sovereign and gracious initiative to redeem his people.

Regarding the human nature the Son assumed, it's best to say that it was unfallen and sinless. Christ's human body and soul had all the capacities of original humanity, thus enabling the Son to experience a fully human life. But Christ's humanity was unfallen and thus not tainted by the transmission or transgression of sin. Over the last two centuries, some have rejected this majority view for the notion that Christ assumed a *fallen* human nature but remained sinless.[19] The motivation for the view is positive: unless the Son assumed our fallenness, he cannot truly redeem us. But it's problematic for at least four reasons.[20]

First, a fallen incarnation lacks biblical support. Expressions such as "born in the likeness of men" (Phil. 2:7), "being

---

19. See Edward Irving, *The Orthodox and Catholic Doctrine of Our Lord's Human Nature, Set Forth in Four Parts* (London: Baldwin & Cradock, 1830); Karl Barth, *Church Dogmatics*, vol. 1, *The Doctrine of the Word of God*, part 2, ed. Geoffrey W. Bromiley and T. F. Torrance, trans. G. T. Thomson and Harold Knight (Edinburgh: T&T Clark, 1956), 153; T. F. Torrance, *Incarnation: The Person and Life of Christ* (Downers Grove, IL: IVP Academic, 2008), 61–62.

20. See Kelly M. Kapic, "The Son's Assumption of a Human Nature: A Call for Clarity," *International Journal of Systematic Theology* 3, no. 2 (2001): 154–66.

found in human form" (Phil. 2:8), and "in the likeness of sinful flesh" (Rom. 8:3) refer to our common human nature, not our corrupt, fallen human nature. The object of the incarnation is always humanity, not sin. Christ came to represent a new humanity. We already have a representative of fallen humanity: the first Adam, in whose transgression we all sinned and came under the penalty of death (Rom. 5:12). In fact, the contrast between the first Adam and Christ as the last Adam makes sense only if Christ does not partake of the corrupted Adamic nature. Jesus is not "in Adam" as we are, and thus he is not fallen.

Second, a "fallen human nature" view seems to imply that corruption is essential to humanity. To argue that unless Christ was fallen, he cannot be fully human like us implies that to be human is to be fallen. No doubt, all humans now are fallen and live in an abnormal, cursed world, but this is an aberration of God's original intent in creating us, which was to bring us to glorification. Fallenness is not essential to us, and thankfully, Christ was fully human yet sinless and unfallen. As such, Christ can become the last Adam, the head of the new creation (2 Cor. 5:17), and in his humanity can redeem us and secure the pattern of our glorified humanity (1 Cor. 15:35–58).

Third, in the case of Christ, a fallen incarnation requires that we separate *fallen* from *sinful*, but this is difficult to warrant biblically and theologically. In Scripture, a fallen nature is the result of sin against God, which places us in a metaphysical and judicial state of sinfulness under God's judgment (Gen. 2:17; Rom. 5:12–21; 6:23; Eph. 2:1–3). But Christ did not exist "in Adam" like us; he came as the last Adam and the head of the new creation to redeem and glorify us.

Fourth, a fallen incarnation risks separating the human nature of Christ from his person. We must maintain that the eternal Son is not fallen, but how do we separate the person from the human nature that he assumed? Would this not imply a Nestorian separation of person and nature so that Christ's humanity is a subject in its own right, acting independently of the Son?

For these reasons, it's better to affirm that Christ's human nature was unfallen and sinless. Our inborn inclination toward rebelling against God was not part of Jesus's human makeup. No doubt, Jesus was fully human and experienced the effects of living in a fallen world, but he did not share the guilt or disposition of Adam's sin passed on to the human race. In fact, Jesus never committed a sin, nor could he (Matt. 3:15; John 8:46; Heb. 4:15; 7:26; 1 Pet. 1:19). Although he was tempted like us, he perfectly obeyed his Father, even unto death, as our covenant mediator, thus accomplishing our salvation as the man Christ Jesus (1 Tim. 2:5; Heb. 5:5–10).

But a question arises: If Jesus could not sin (i.e., he was impeccable), were his temptations genuine? Although Jesus did not sin, must he not have been able to do so to be like us? How was his obedience truly *human* obedience? Three points are helpful to answer this important question.

First, Jesus was genuinely tempted yet "without sin" (Heb. 4:15). As the obedient Son, he faced trials, temptations, and sufferings for us from the beginning of his ministry to his death on the cross (Luke 4:1–13; 22:39–46). Yet this does not mean that his temptations were identical to ours in every respect. Why? Although Jesus is fully human, he is also the divine Son, and his temptations reflect this fact. For example, Jesus was tempted to turn rocks into bread (not something we are tempted with), thus using his divine power instead of obeying his Father's will to render human obedience for us as the last Adam (Heb. 2:5–18; 5:8–10; cf. Rom. 5:12–21).

Also, unlike us, Jesus was not tempted by anything within or internal to himself. He was not enticed by sinful desires contrary to God's creational and moral norms since there was no sin in him, not even a predisposition to sin, given the sanctifying work of the Spirit. Rather, Jesus was tempted by normal sinless human weaknesses and external forces. He could be tempted through hunger, through fear of pain, and, as Donald Macleod observes, through "holy affections, feelings and longings which, in the course of his work, he had to thwart."[21] Foremost among these desires was his perfect fellowship with his Father by the Spirit. In Gethsemane, Jesus was overwhelmed by what lay before him, but "he was not being called upon to mortify a lust. He was being called upon to frustrate the holiest aspiration of which man is capable. What he wanted and what his Father directed were in conflict. Hence the 'loud cries and tears' (Heb. 5:7)."[22] In fact, we can say that Jesus's temptations were not only genuine, they were more real than we could ever imagine or experience, since he never yielded to temptation as we do. He unswervingly and joyfully obeyed his Father's will at great cost for our salvation.

Second, Jesus is impeccable because he is the divine Son who assumed a human nature, and as such, his human nature never existed apart from this union. Jesus, then, is not merely another Adam (constituted by a human person and nature); he is the last Adam, the head of the new creation, the eternal Son incarnate. And as the Son, it's impossible for him to sin and to yield to temptation because God cannot sin. As Macleod rightly notes, "If he sinned, God sinned. At this level, the impeccability of Christ is absolute. It rests not upon his unique endowment with the Spirit nor upon the indefectibility of God's redemp-

---

21. Donald Macleod, *The Person of Christ*, Contours of Christian Theology (Downers Grove, IL: InterVarsity Press, 1998), 226.

22. Macleod, *Person of Christ*, 226.

tive purpose, but upon the fact that he is who he is."[23] Bavinck makes the same point:

> He is the Son of God, the Logos, who was in the beginning with God and himself God. He is one with the Father and always carries out his Father's will and work. For those who confess this of Christ, the possibility of him sinning and falling is unthinkable.[24]

In fact, it is this truth that both grounds our assurance that God's glorious plan cannot fail and explains why the last Adam is far greater than the first.

The church made theological sense of this reasoning by employing the concepts of *anhypostasia* and *enhypostasia*, as discussed in chapter 6. Building on the person-nature distinction and affirming that Christ's human nature consisted of a human body and soul, *anhypostasia* taught that the Son assumed a human nature "without a human person" or "a human 'I.'" Christ's human nature, then, had no independent human subsistence other than "in the person" (*enhypostasia*) of the Son, by whom it was assumed and to whom it was joined. The divine Son is the only self-conscious, self-asserting subject of Christ. The Trinitarian Son, who eternally possesses and shares the divine nature with the Father and the Spirit, assumed a human nature and now subsists, lives, and acts forever in both natures, hence the ultimate reason why Jesus is impeccable.

Third, although Jesus is impeccable, owing to his divine person, we must still explain *how* his temptations are real. Part of the explanation is defining the nature of human freedom properly. Many who reject Christ's impeccability often assume that for Christ to be truly tempted, he must always have the "ability

23. Macleod, *Person of Christ*, 229–30.
24. Bavinck, *Sin and Salvation in Christ*, 314.

to do otherwise," namely, sin. But this assumes a libertarian view of freedom, which is problematic for numerous reasons.[25] Instead, if one adopts a compatibilistic view of freedom, one can make sense of how Jesus impeccably resists temptation *freely* since he always chooses according to his unfallen, sinless wants and desires.

Furthermore, we must remember that even though Christ was unfallen and impeccable, the Son, as our covenant representative, had to render *human* obedience for us. The Son's action in and through his human nature did not change the integrity of that nature; he lived, acted, and faced every temptation as a true man to redeem us. And as Scripture wonderfully reminds us, it's for this reason that Jesus has not only secured our eternal salvation but has also become our merciful, faithful, and sympathetic Savior (Heb. 2:18; 4:14–16).

At this point, it is also crucial to stress the work of the Spirit on the human nature of Christ. Jesus is impeccable because he is the eternal Son who subsists and acts in both natures, but it is also because of his reliance on the Spirit at work in him that Jesus did not sin. From Jesus's conception, the Spirit sanctified, gifted, and empowered the Son in his humanity, and Jesus, throughout his entire life, obeyed for us as a man by the Spirit. All this entails that Jesus's temptations were genuine although he was impeccable. As the sinless one who could not sin, he still had to choose to forgo his rights and privileges for us (Heb. 12:2–3). He had to choose to go to the cross even though he knew the cost. But by doing so, he perfectly fulfilled the Father's will by the Spirit, secured our redemption, and in his humanity became the pattern of our glorified humanity (1 Cor. 15:45–49).

---

25. For a defense of compatibilism, see John S. Feinberg, *No One Like Him: The Doctrine of God*, Foundations of Evangelical Theology (Wheaton, IL: Crossway, 2001), 625–775; John M. Frame, *The Doctrine of God*, Theology of Lordship (Phillipsburg, NJ: P&R, 2002), 119–59.

The Two Natures

7. In the incarnation, the eternal Son took on a new mode of existence as a man. The divine Son now subsists and acts in two natures without changing the integrity of either nature, confusing them, or melding them into a divine-human hybrid. The Son's action in his human nature, then, does not override the limitations of that nature: the Son truly lives, experiences the world, and acts as a man.

8. Given the ontological priority of God the Son, in the incarnation the Son was not limited to acting through his human nature alone since he continued to act through his divine nature, as he has from eternity.

The next two statements help us think through the action of the divine Son in both natures. In assuming a human nature, the divine Son becomes visibly present in a new mode of existence as a man. In and through his human nature, the Son lives and acts within the normal physical, mental, volitional, and psychological capacities of an unfallen, sinless human nature. As the Son, he experienced the wonder and weaknesses of a human life. He grew in wisdom and physical stature (Luke 2:52), experienced tears and joy, and suffered death and a glorious resurrection for his people and their salvation (John 11:33, 35; 19:30; 1 Cor. 15:3–4).

The same Son who experiences these things as a man, however, also continues to live and act as he has done from eternity as God the Son in relation with the Father and the Spirit. This truth is taught in Scripture's affirmation that the incarnate Son continues to uphold the universe (Col. 1:16–17; Heb. 1:3), even as he continues to perform other divine actions throughout his life and ministry. In Christ, there are two natures that remain distinct and retain their own attributes and integrity, yet the Son is able to act through both natures. The Son, then, is not completely circumscribed by his human nature; he is also able to act "outside" (*extra*) his human nature in his divine nature, as he has always done. The Son, who has always acted inseparably from the Father and by the Spirit, continues to do so, but now, as a result of the incarnation, he also acts as a man—indeed, as the obedient Son for us and our salvation. In the incarnation, the Son's full deity and humanity are not diminished.

To make sense of Christ's dual action, theology has employed the resources of *enhypostasia*, the *communicatio idiomatum*, and the *extra*, as discussed in chapter 6. Let us briefly comment on these interlocking truths as we think about the action of the divine Son in the incarnation.

Enhypostatic *Union and Christ's Dual Agency*

In the incarnation, the divine Son "personalized" the human nature created for him by triune action. The Son did not become or replace a human person but assumed a human body-soul composite into his metaphysical identity "without a (human) person" (*anhypostasia*). Thus, when Jesus speaks, thinks, wills, and acts, he does so as the eternal Son through both natures.

As applied to Christ's deity, *enhypostasia* entails that the divine Son never ceases to exercise his divine prerogatives in relation to the Father and the Spirit. For example, the Son, even after the incarnation, continues to "[uphold] the universe by the word of his power" (Heb. 1:3), because "in him all things hold together" (Col. 1:17). Contrary to various forms of kenoticism, the Son did not set aside certain divine attributes or their exercise when he assumed a human nature. The perfections of the divine nature cannot change, and the person of the incarnate Son continues to subsist in and act through the divine nature.

As applied to Christ's humanity, *enhypostasia* entails that the divine Son is now visibly present in the human nature he assumed. The Son does not subsist *by* the human nature, since he is God the Son; instead, he subsists *in* the human nature he has assumed. And as such, the Son lives and acts as a man without changing the integrity of his human nature. For this reason, the Son experiences life as a man: he grows in his body, gains wisdom, laughs, cries, suffers, bears our sin, dies, and is raised for us. And by his obedience, he secures our eternal redemption as our covenant head precisely because the one who obeys for us in life and death is the divine Son.

The Communicatio Idiomatum *and Christ's Dual Agency*

Alongside the emphasis on the unity of Christ's person (*enhypostasia*), it is also necessary to affirm that the two natures remain distinct and retain their own integrity, thus upholding the Creator-creature distinction even in the hypostatic union of Christ's deity and humanity. Theology has used the concept of the *communicatio idiomatum* ("the communication of attributes") to explain this relationship. Although theologians have different conceptions of the *communicatio*, they typically agree on two points: (1) each nature retained its own attributes, and (2) the attributes of each nature may be predicated of the Son since he is the person of both natures. The *communicatio* is vital for making sense of seemingly contradictory biblical data, and it helps in thinking through Christ's dual agency.

For example, Scripture teaches Jesus's eternal existence and his birth; it also teaches Jesus's omnipotence and weariness. By employing the *communicatio*, we can say that the former in both cases applies to the Son in his deity, while the latter applies to the Son in his humanity.

Or consider Christ's knowledge. Not only does Scripture teach that Jesus grew in wisdom (Luke 2:52), Jesus also said that he did not know the timing of the end (Matt. 24:36; Mark 13:32). But if Jesus was the divine Son, then how did he not know when the end would come? The *communicatio* is helpful in answering this question. The Son in his deity knows all things according to the triune eternally ordered person relations within God, yet the Son through his human nature experienced growth in knowledge as a man within the limits of that nature. In his humanity, the Son gained knowledge as humans gain it: by revelation, both general and special. In fact, in the case of Christ, on this point, it's crucial to stress Scripture's emphasis on the Spirit's work in Christ's human nature. It's the Spirit who creates and sanctifies Christ's human nature and fills it with grace beyond measure (John 3:34). No doubt, the Spirit's work does not transgress the limits of that nature, yet as Macleod notes, Jesus's capacity for revelatory knowledge by the Spirit is different from ordinary men, given his sinlessness and his unique relation to the Father and the Spirit. As Macleod suggests, "[Jesus's] intellect was perfectly attuned to the divine,"[26] and he "conversed with God as his Son; and he thought as his Son. We may even say that he lived in a thought-world of pure revelation so that to an extent that we cannot fathom God disclosed himself not only to his thinking but *in* his thinking."[27] Yet the Son, acting and knowing as a man, functioned within the limits of his human capacities, including his human mind and will, and thus truly grew in knowledge as a man.

Does this entail that Jesus was ever ignorant of something he ought to have known? Can we appeal to Jesus's human knowledge to argue that his knowledge was only a first-century un-

---

26. Macleod, *Person of Christ*, 167.
27. Macleod, *Person of Christ*, 167; emphasis original.

derstanding and thus that he made mistakes? No, for at least two reasons. First, as mediator, Jesus was "never ignorant of anything that he ought to have known."[28] As a man, Jesus grew in knowledge, but as mediator, he knew all that he needed to know, and he lived and acted in obedience to his Father's will by the Spirit. Second, as mediator, Jesus "had to fulfill his office of Mediator within the limitations of a human body, so he had to fulfill it within the limitations of a human mind."[29] Yet none of this implies fallibility in his mediatorial office. All that it entails is that the incarnate Son, in relation to the divine persons and in his divine mission to redeem us, knew what he needed to know and spoke with divine authority as the Son because all that he said was from the Father and by the Spirit, so that his actions and words are also the actions and words of God.

Or consider Christ's death (Luke 23:46; 1 Cor. 15:3). By applying the *communicatio*, we can say that the Son died through his human nature, which entailed the separation of his human body and soul. In death, the Son did not cease to exist but continued to subsist in the divine nature and in his human soul; the hypostatic union was never severed even in death. But as a man, the Son did experience death such that he purchased the church "with his own blood" (Acts 20:28). God does not have blood to shed. But what is true of Christ's human nature is also true of the divine Son.

Or consider the question of God's impassibility related to Christ's death. Once again, the *communicatio* helps us think through this issue. Christ suffered on the cross, but this does not undermine divine impassibility. As Cyril of Alexandria once said, "The impassible suffered."[30] Why? First, the person of the

---

28. Macleod, *Person of Christ*, 168.
29. Macleod, *Person of Christ*, 169.
30. Quoted in Thomas G. Weinandy, *Does God Suffer?* (Notre Dame, IN: University of Notre Dame Press, 2000), 202.

Son suffered as a man through the human nature he assumed, not through the divine nature. Second, the Son suffered, not the Father or the Spirit. All three divine persons act inseparably, yet specific acts terminate on each person according to their *ad intra* mode of subsistence in the divine nature. In the case of the incarnation, it's only the Son, not the Father or the Spirit, who assumes a human nature and in that nature suffers and dies. Yet it's also true that prior to the incarnation, as Thomas Weinandy notes, "God, who is impassible in himself, never experienced and knew suffering and death as a man *in a human manner.*"[31] But now the Son can experience human life, suffering, and death as a man. Gloriously, the Son is not changed in becoming a man because he has always existed in the fullness of divine life. But now, in his humanity, the divine Son suffers and dies as an expression of his own sovereign choice to obey the Father's will to accomplish our eternal salvation.

The use of *enhypostasia* and the *communicatio* helps make sense of Christ's dual agency. Critics often charge classic Christology with predicating contradictory attributes to one and the same person, but these two theological concepts remind us that this is incorrect. We are not predicating contradictory attributes of the same person *in exactly the same way*. The Son is truly omnipotent, omniscient, omnipresent, and eternal because what is true of the divine nature is true of the Son (the person), who subsists in the divine nature. The Son, however, also subsists in a human nature. So we must duplicate the predication of attributes to the Son, this time according to his human nature. The Son, then, is weak, unknowing, and spatially and temporally located because what is true of a human nature is true of the Son, who subsists in that nature. No doubt, we are left with plenty of unknowns regarding Christological metaphysics, yet

---

31. Weinandy, *Does God Suffer?*, 206; emphasis original.

there is no logical contradiction. All there is, is worship and wonder for such a glorious Redeemer who meets our every need. Yet one more piece is needed to round out our discussion of Christ's dual action as the incarnate Son.

The Extra *and Christ's Dual Agency*

As a result of the incarnation, the divine Son acts through two natures without violating the integrity of either one. In his human nature, the Son is limited to the capacities of a sinless human nature as gifted and empowered by the Spirit. But the Son also continues to live and act "outside" (*extra*) his human nature according to the perfections of the divine nature.

The concept of the *extra* has been employed to make sense of this thinking. Since the Creator has ontological priority over anything creaturely, the divine Son has ontological priority over his human nature and thus continues to have a divine life "outside" it. Contrary to a common caricature, the *extra* does not diminish Christ's humanity; it preserves it. From conception on, the Son humbled himself by assuming a human nature with its limitations and living a new mode of existence as man. Yet the Son did not change regarding his deity, triune relations, and agency. The Son continued to act as he has always acted, namely, "outside" the reality of human life, yet now he is also able to act through his human nature. In fact, when the *extra* is combined with *krypsis*, a clearer understanding of Christ's *kenosis* is gained: the incarnation brought a real concealment but not an abdication of the eternal Son's divine majesty. The Son, in a new way, became one with us to redeem us, while also remaining who he has always been from eternity.

Given the Creator-creature and person-nature distinctions, it's not contradictory to assert that the Son simultaneously acts through both natures to accomplish works consistent with each nature. The Son's action in both natures is not mutually exclusive, although difficult to conceive. As humans, we are human persons subsisting in human natures. We are not divine persons, and we do not subsist in two different natures. Conceiving of how one person performs actions according to both natures surpasses our comprehension, yet it's wonderfully true. The concepts of *enhypostasia*, the *communicatio*, and the *extra* help us make sense of the Bible's majestic presentation of our Lord Jesus Christ.

A New Covenant Head

9. By assuming a human nature, the divine Son became the first man of the new creation, perfectly qualified to be our great mediator and new covenant head.

As the Son incarnate, our Lord Jesus Christ became the first man of the new creation, our great mediator and new covenant head. As this man, he reverses the work of the first Adam and forges ahead as the last Adam, our great trailblazer and champion (Gk. *archēgon*, Heb. 2:10). Owing to the incarnation, God the Son becomes perfectly qualified to meet our every need, especially our need for the forgiveness of sin (Jer. 31:34; Heb. 7:22–28; 9:15–10:18). According to the Bible's storyline, only the incarnate Son could mediate the reconciliation of the triune Creator–covenant God and humans by offering himself as a sinless, sufficient, substitutionary sacrifice such that God himself redeems his people as a man (1 Tim. 2:5–6; Heb. 5–10). As the divine Son, Christ alone satisfies God's own judgment on sinful humanity and demand for perfect obedience (Rom. 5:12–21). As the incarnate Son, Christ alone identifies with us as our representative and substitute (Heb. 5:1). Our salvation hope for the payment of our sin and our full restoration as God's image bearers and priest-sons is accomplished only by our Lord Jesus Christ (Rom. 3:21–26; Heb. 2:5–18). As J. I. Packer explains,

> Without incarnation there would have been no God-man, and without the God-man there would have been no mediation, no revelation of redemption. . . . The enfleshing of the Son was thus integral to God's plan of salvation, and the glory of Christ's unique person must be seen as an aspect of the glory of the Gospel itself.[32]

Lord and Savior

10. Jesus the Messiah, God the Son incarnate, is unique and alone Lord and Savior and thus demands our entire lives in faith, love, and obedience to him.[33]

Jesus is in a category all by himself. Given who the triune God is in all his glory, aseity, and moral perfection, and given what sin is before God, it's no wonder that apart from the divine Son's incarnation and his entire work for us, there is no salvation (John 14:6; Acts 4:11).

For this reason, it's not enough merely to state correctly who Jesus is according to Scripture and the church's confessions, as important as that is. Given who Jesus is, we must also be led to worship, faith in him alone, proclamation, and a glad and willing submission to his lordship in every area of our lives. In Jesus, we see the Lord of glory, who has taken on flesh to become our all-sufficient Redeemer. By sharing our common

---

32. J. I. Packer, "The Glory of the Person of Christ," in *The Glory of Christ*, ed. John H. Armstrong (Wheaton, IL: Crossway, 2002), 54.

33. Parts of this section are adapted from Stephen J. Wellum, "Christological Reflections in Light of Scripture's Covenants," *Southern Baptist Journal of Theology* 16, no. 2 (2012): 79–107; Wellum, "*Solus Christus*: What the Reformers Taught and Why It Still Matters," *Southern Baptist Journal of Theology* 19, no. 4 (2015): 79–107. Used by permission of *The Southern Baptist Journal of Theology*.

human nature, the divine Son is now able to do a work that we could never do. In his incarnation and cross work, we see the resolution of the triune God to take on himself our guilt and sin so that the horrible effects of sin are reversed and his own moral demand is fully satisfied. In Christ alone, we see the triune God making this world right by the ratification of a new covenant in his blood. In Jesus Christ, we see the perfectly obedient Son take the initiative to keep his covenant promises by assuming our human nature, veiling his glory, and achieving for us our eternal salvation.

Our Savior and Redeemer is unique in both who he is and what he does. In fact, because sin makes our plight so desperate, the only person who can save us is God's own dear Son. It's only as the Son incarnate that our Lord can represent us, pay for our sin, and stand in our place. Only Jesus can satisfy God's righteous demands against us since he is one with the Lord as God the Son; only Jesus can do this for us because he is truly a man and can represent us. Representation requires identification, and in all these ways, our Lord is perfectly suited to meet our every need. Without the incarnation and Christ's entire obedient work, there is no salvation for us. To turn Gotthold Lessing's words (see p. 23) on their head, Jesus is a historical particular who has absolute universal significance for us, and apart from saving faith in him and him alone, we stand under God's judgment and condemnation.

But for us to appreciate this truth, another critical point needs to be stressed. It is often said that Christianity is a sinner's religion: we do not understand, know, and adore Jesus correctly unless we have come, by God's grace, first to see that we are lost and condemned before God. It is not until we see that our greatest need as humans is that we need to be justified before the triune holy God that we gladly embrace the Jesus of the Bible as our Lord and Savior.

This is something our secular, postmodern culture does not understand, given its rejection of Christian theology and adoption of false ideologies. Mark it well, however: to understand the Jesus of the Bible correctly, to come to know him rightly, and to place all our confidence in him personally, we must also come to know something of our own guilt before God and why it is that we need the kind of Redeemer he is. For it is not until we know ourselves as lost, under the sentence of death, and condemned before God, that we can even appreciate and rejoice in a divine-human Redeemer. It is only when we realize that we cannot save ourselves that we clearly see that he is the Redeemer we need. And for people who by God's grace come to see their need of him, the Jesus of the Bible is more than a doctrine to state; he is the only Lord and Savior to be embraced, loved, adored, and obeyed.

9

Recovering the Centrality of Christ

Who do we say that Jesus is? Why is he important? Why do Scripture and the church confess that Christ is unique, exclusive, and the only Lord and Savior? This book has sought to answer some of these questions from Scripture and the confessional orthodoxy of the church. And in light of Scripture's teaching, we finish this book where we began: there is no greater need for the church today than to think rightly about Jesus biblically and theologically. The life and health of the church depends on a correct Christology, rooted and grounded in an accurate theology proper—yet not merely a Christology confessed but one that leads us to faith, trust, and confidence in our Lord Jesus and to an entire life lived in adoration, praise, and obedience to the triune God.

The reason why this is so should be obvious if we have understood what Scripture teaches regarding our triune God in the face of the incarnate Son. Given that Jesus is the divine Son, the eternal "Word made flesh" (cf. John 1:1, 14), in him alone is life and life eternal (John 17:3). Repeatedly, Scripture reminds us that in Christ alone, all God's sovereign purposes find their fulfillment (Heb. 1:1–3). As Paul beautifully reminds us, in Christ alone, God's eternal plan is to bring "all things," "things in heaven and things on earth," under Christ's headship (Eph. 1:9–10), which has already begun in his first coming and which will be consummated in his return. Jesus, the incarnate divine Son, is central to God's eternal plan and new creation work. Indeed, as Paul again reminds us in his famous Christological hymn, not only is the eternal Son the one through whom the Father has created, but also, the very purpose of creation is ultimately "for him" (Col. 1:16).

Given the centrality of Christ in Scripture and theology, it's not surprising that to misidentify him is so serious. In fact, as Jeremy Jackson rightly reminds us, at the heart of *all* heresy and false understandings of the gospel and Christian theology is a distortion or denial of Christ.[1] In many ways, one's Christology is a test case for one's entire theology. The more our Christology is off, especially in terms of the Son's unique, exclusive identity and all-sufficient work, the more our theology will be wrong in other areas. "Ideas have consequences," and the most central "idea" to get right is who Jesus is vis-à-vis the triune God. There are many beliefs that distinguish Christianity from other worldviews but none as central and significant as who Jesus is.

Thinking through all that Scripture says about Jesus and wrestling with the church as she has sought to faithfully confess Christ is not an easy task, but it's absolutely necessary, especially if we are going to think rightly about God, the gospel, and the entire Christian faith. The study of Christology is not reserved for academic theologians; it's the privilege, responsi-

---

1. See Jeremy C. Jackson, *No Other Foundation: The Church through Twenty Centuries* (Westchester, IL: Crossway, 1980), 31–42.

bility, and glory of every Christian. The Christian life and the Christian ministry are about knowing God in truth, believing and obeying God's Word in our lives, and being vigilant for the truth of the gospel by "destroy[ing] arguments and every lofty opinion raised against the knowledge of God, and tak[ing] every thought captive to obey Christ" (2 Cor. 10:5).

Yet although Scripture and theology remind us about the centrality of Christ in everything, the evangelical church, sadly, is in danger of neglecting this truth. Evidence for this concern is found in the 2018 *State of Theology* report, which reveals a serious lack of biblical-theological knowledge and fidelity.[2] But further evidence is found in whatever seems to be the latest discussion on social media. The evangelical church seems more willing to "fight" and "divide" over issues that are entailments of the gospel than to stand faithfully for truths that are central to the gospel, namely, Christology and theology proper, as evidenced in the *State of Theology* poll.

My goal in writing this book is to call the church back to what is central: the glory of Christ. My hope is that this volume will help equip the church to know better the basic scriptural data regarding Christ and the church's theological confession of him. My prayer is that in spending time thinking through the glory and majesty of our Lord Jesus Christ, readers of this book will be led, in some small way, to a renewed delight to know and proclaim Christ and him alone (Col. 1:28). Indeed, the church first exists to know and proclaim the glory of the triune God in the face of Christ, and a move away from this center will lead the church away from life and health.

One of Scripture's culminating visions is Revelation 4–5. It is a breathtaking vision in which the triune God is seen in all

---

2. See *The State of Theology*, Ligonier, accessed May 7, 2020, http://thestateof theology.com.

his glory, holiness, authority, sovereignty, and self-sufficiency. In this vision, we are reminded about what is truly central and important: the Lord on his throne and the Lamb who was slain. In every generation, Christians need this vision to renew them. We need to be reminded about who is central, who is worthy, who is to be obeyed, and who is our only hope and salvation. As a result of thinking through the glory of our Lord Jesus in Scripture and theology, may we be led to confess with the angelic hosts:

> To him who sits on the throne and to the Lamb
> be blessing and honor and glory and might forever
>   and ever!" (Rev. 5:13)

Glossary

ad extra. In Trinitarian theology, this Latin term refers to the works of the triune God "outside" (*extra*) himself, in creation, providence, revelation, redemption, and judgment. In these divine works, all three persons, Father, Son, and Holy Spirit, act inseparably as the one God yet distinctly according to their relations of persons within the Trinity.

ad intra. In Trinitarian theology, this Latin term refers to God's life "within" (*intra*) himself prior to his outward works and within the eternal, necessary person relations of the Father, Son, and Holy Spirit. Each of the three persons is fully God, sharing fully and equally the one undivided divine nature, yet they are distinguished according to their relations of persons within the Trinity: paternity (Father), eternal generation (Son), and eternal procession (Spirit).

adoptionism. An early church heresy that denied the deity of Christ. There are variations of the view, but overall, it teaches that Jesus was a mere man on whom the "Christ" (God's power and presence) came at his baptism. By this act and owing to his life, death, and resurrection, Jesus was "adopted" in time as God's son and given unique powers. Jesus is not, however, the eternal Son of God, who in time assumed a human nature and who is now fully God and fully human.

anhypostasia and *enhypostasia.* In Christology, these Greek terms refer to the nature of the hypostatic union. In the incarnation, the eternal Son, who shares the divine nature with the Father and the Spirit, assumed a human nature (body and "rational soul," with such corresponding capacities as a mind, a will, and emotions) and became the subject of both his divine and human natures. *Anhypostasia* emphasizes that the divine Son assumed a human nature "without" (*an-*) a human person or subject (*hypostasis*), while *enhypostasia* reminds us that Christ's human nature is never without a person because it subsists "in" (*en-*) the person (*hypostasis*) of the divine Son. The eternal Son of God is the person or subject of both natures.

Apollinarianism. An early church heresy, associated with Apollinarius (ca. 310–390), that compromised the full humanity of Christ in the incarnation. Apollinarius taught that a human nature consists of three parts: a human body, a soul, and a spirit (or "mind," Gk. *nous*). In the incarnation, the divine Son replaced the human spirit (or "mind," Gk. *nous*) and assumed only a human body, which resulted in an incomplete human nature, thus making it different from ours. It was rejected by the church at the Councils of Constantinople (381) and Chalcedon (451).

Arianism. An early church heresy, associated with Arius (ca. 256–336), that denies the eternality and deity of Christ. According to Trinitarian theology, Arianism is Unitarian, since it views the Son as the first and greatest created being through whom God created the world, but the Son is not of the same nature as the Father. This view was rejected by the church at the Council of Nicaea (325) and at subsequent ecumenical councils, including Chalcedon (451). The church affirmed that the Son is God and thus of the "same nature" (*homoousios*) as the Father.

Chalcedonian Definition. The church's definitive statement from the Council of Chalcedon (451) on the identity of Christ. It affirms that Jesus is the eternal, divine Son in relation to the Father and the Spirit, who by adding a human nature (a human body and "rational soul") to himself is now and forever God the Son incarnate. The confession of Chalcedon is that Jesus is one person (the divine Son) who now subsists in two natures and thus is fully God and fully man. The Chalcedonian Definition also rejected all previous heresies of the church regarding who Jesus is, including Arianism, Apollinarianism, Nestorianism, and Monophysitism.

Christology from above versus Christology from below. These expressions refer to different approaches taken by people in formulating a Christology or stating who Jesus is. For some, *from above* refers to doing a Christology by starting with Christ's deity, while *from below* starts with his humanity. It is best, however, to think of *from above* as referring to the doing of Christology by starting with the full authority, teaching, and theology of Scripture, while *from below* does Christology within the confines of the historical-critical method.

communicatio idiomatum (**"the communication of attributes"**). This Latin phrase teaches that whatever may be said of Christ's divine and human nature may be said of the person of the Son. For example, Jesus can say, "Before Abraham was, I am" (John 8:58), which means that he is the eternal, divine Son; thus, whatever is true of his divine nature is true of his person. At the same time, Jesus can say, "I thirst" (John 19:28), which refers to his humanity; thus, whatever is true of his human nature is true of his person. In this way, in Christ the Creator-creature distinction is preserved, while a true incarnation has resulted in the Son (the person) being the subject of both natures and living and acting through both natures.

Dyothelitism versus Monothelitism. Classic, orthodox Christology affirms that as a result of the incarnation, Christ has two wills (Gk. *dyo*, "two"; *thelēma*, "will"), a divine and a human will located in each respective nature. This view was affirmed at the Third Council of Constantinople (680–681), which also rejected Monothelitism (Gk. *monos*, "one"; *thelēma*, "will"), a view that locates the will in the person of the Son. The church rejected Monothelitism because it entails three wills in the Trinity and also denies a human will in Christ.

extra [*Calvinisticum*]**, the.** The teaching that in the incarnation, Jesus not only retained his divine attributes but also continued to exercise them as the Trinitarian Son. Given that the Son now subsists in two natures, he is still able to live a divine life "outside" (*extra*) his human nature. The human nature of Christ, in other words, does not circumscribe his divine life. In the Reformation, the view was associated with John Calvin by the Lutherans, but it is simply a truth taught by classic, orthodox Christology through the ages.

impeccability versus peccability. These terms refer to the question whether the incarnate Son could have sinned, while also affirming that Jesus did not actually sin. Impeccability (Lat. *in-*, "not"; *peccare*, "to sin") affirms that Jesus could not have sinned, owing to the union of his divine and human nature in the person of the Son. Because the Son is God in eternal relation to the Father and the Spirit, although when acting in and through his human nature he is human, he, the Son, could not sin. Peccability affirms that Jesus could have sinned but did not actually sin.

intratextual versus extratextual reading of Scripture. These expressions are related to different approaches to Christology, namely, the doing of Christology from above and from below. As such, they refer to one's method in approaching Scripture and drawing Christological conclusions. *Intratextual* refers to approaching Scripture according to its own claims, authority, teaching, and theology and thus starting from above. Conversely, *extratextual* refers to approaching Scripture in light of some "outside" (*extra*) view that functions as more authoritative than Scripture and by which Scripture is interpreted, thus starting from below. Classic, orthodox Christology follows an intratextual approach, while various historical reconstructions of Jesus follow an extratextual approach.

kenoticism (kenotic Christology). Often associated with nineteenth-century German and English theology, this view argues that in the incarnation, the divine Son either temporarily or permanently divested himself of his nonessential attributes inconsistent with a human life, such as omnipresence, omnipotence, and omniscience. *Kenotic* derives from Philippians 2:7 and the Greek word *kenoō*, "to empty." This view has been rejected by classic, orthodox Christology as not only undermining the deity of the Son but also rendering problematic the doctrine of the Trinity and the biblical teaching regarding the incarnation of the divine Son of God.

modalism. An early church heresy that affirms the unity of God but denies that the divine persons, Father, Son, and Holy Spirit, are distinct persons who share the same undivided divine nature. This view insists that the terms *Father*, *Son*, and *Holy Spirit* are three "names" for, or "modes" of, the same person but not terms that refer to three distinct divine persons. Modalism is a form of Monarchianism that rightly affirms God's unity (Gk. *monos*, "one"; *archos*, "ruler, source") but denies the coequality and distinctness of the divine persons.

Monophysitism (Eutychianism). An early church heresy that denies that Christ has two distinct natures—a divine and a human nature—united in the person of the Son. It is associated with Eutyches (ca. 380–456), and it was condemned at the Council of Chalcedon (451). Monophysitism (Gk. *monos*, "one"; *physis*, "nature") teaches that as a result of the incarnation, Christ's human nature was taken up, absorbed, and merged into his divine nature, so that both natures were changed into one new nature—a kind of third nature that is neither fully divine nor fully human.

nature (Gk. *ousia*; Lat. *essentia, substantia*). In theology, a "nature" refers to what a thing is. In regard to God, a divine nature is what God is, often described in terms of his attributes, which are all essential to him. Thus, the nature of God is simple, infinite, eternal, immaterial, omnipotent, omniscient, omnipresent, and so on—and necessarily so. In regard to humans, a human nature is what humans are, often described in terms of a body-soul composite with corresponding capacities, such as will, mind, and emotions.

Nestorianism. An early church heresy that affirms that Christ has two persons and that fails to account for the unity of Christ's person. It is associated with Nestorius (ca. 386–451), and it was condemned at the Council of Ephesus (431). Nestorianism views Christ's humanity as if it were an independent man or subject, which opens the door to adoptionism. Contrary to Nestorianism, Scripture insists that Christ's human nature is not an independent human person but a single person, the divine Son, who acts as a unified subject now in two natures.

Nicene Creed. The church's Trinitarian confession of God along with the confession of the deity of the Son, our Lord

Jesus Christ. The Nicene Creed is a compilation of the first two church councils, Nicaea (325) and Constantinople (381). The creed rejects Arianism and affirms that the Son is "begotten of the Father" (eternal generation) and of the "same nature" (*homoousios*) as the Father, and thus fully God. It also affirms that the Holy Spirit is "the Lord and Giver of life," a distinct divine person alongside the Father and Son.

person (Gk. *hypostasis*; Lat. *persona, subsistentia*). In regard to the Trinity, this term applies to the Father, Son, and Holy Spirit, who share the same undivided essence yet are distinguished by their relations, or mode of subsistence in the divine nature. The Father is characterized by "paternity," the Son is characterized by "sonship" and is from the Father, and the Holy Spirit is characterized by "procession" and eternally proceeds from the Father and the Son. In regard to Christology, the Son is the second person of the Godhead, who at the incarnation assumed a human nature. The person is the subject of the nature, and in the case of Christ, the person of the Son is the subject of both natures.

quests for the historical Jesus. An approach to Christology that is done from below and within the confines of Enlightenment and post-Enlightenment thought. It began in 1778 and continues today; in fact, there are three distinct manifestations of it. The quests are pursuits to discover who Jesus really was—the "Jesus of history"—over against the Jesus revealed in Scripture. The quests assume that the Jesus of the Bible is not necessarily the Jesus of history, so by following the historical-critical method and what is called methodological naturalism, they seek to uncover the "real" Jesus. Methodological naturalism is the view that in our study of history, we assume that divine, supernatural agency is not at work, and we explain everything in terms of "natural" cause-and-effect relationships.

taxis. In Trinitarian theology, this Greek term refers to the necessary, eternal, and unchanging relations of persons, or "ordering," between the Father, Son, and Holy Spirit. The Father is first, has paternity owing to his relation to the Son, and is the one who initiates and sends. The Son is distinguished from the Father since he is eternally from the Father. The Spirit is neither the Father nor the Son since he eternally proceeds from the Father and the Son. In God's external acts, all three persons act inseparably yet distinctly according to their *taxis*, or "ordered" relations.

Further Reading

Athanasius, *On the Incarnation*. Translated by John Behr. Popular Patristics 44b. Yonkers, NY: St. Vladimir's Seminary Press, 2011. A classic work from the patristic era that clearly expounds the glory of Christ and the nature of the incarnation from Scripture.

Bauckham, Richard. *Jesus and the God of Israel: "God Crucified" and Other Studies on the New Testament's Christology of Divine Identity*. Grand Rapids, MI: Eerdmans, 2008. An advanced work that discusses current debates within biblical and theological studies on who Jesus is and that defends a high Christology of Jesus's divine identity.

Letham, Robert. *The Message of the Person of Christ: The Word Made Flesh*. The Bible Speaks Today. Downers Grove, IL: IVP Academic, 2013. An introductory book that works through key biblical texts in the Old and New Testaments to reveal who the Jesus of the Bible is. A must-read for those who want to learn how to preach Christology from Scripture and move from text to theological formulation.

Macleod, Donald. *The Person of Christ*. Contours of Christian Theology. Downers Grove, IL: InterVarsity Press, 1998. A helpful, more advanced, and classic treatment of the person of Christ that works through biblical, historical, and systematic theology.

Morgan, Christopher W., and Robert A. Peterson, eds. *The Deity of Christ*. Theology in Community. Wheaton, IL: Crossway,

2011. A more advanced book, written by eight scholars, that expounds and defends the deity of Christ in Scripture and history and its application to our current age.

Nichols, Stephen J. *For Us and for Our Salvation: The Doctrine of Christ in the Early Church*. Wheaton, IL: Crossway, 2007. An introductory and helpful work covering the development of Christology and the discussion of key theologians who helped formulate orthodoxy in the first five centuries of the church.

Vos, Geerhardus. *Christology*. Vol. 3 of *Reformed Dogmatics*. Translated and edited by Richard B. Gaffin Jr. Bellingham, WA: Lexham, 2014. A midlevel book designed to cover the basic biblical and historical material concerning who Jesus is and what the nature of the incarnation is by working through various questions and answers.

Wellum, Stephen J. *God the Son Incarnate: The Doctrine of Christ*. Foundations of Evangelical Theology. Wheaton, IL: Crossway, 2016. An advanced book that seeks to describe and defend Chalcedonian Christology in light of current issues and theological trends.

General Index

Scripture Index

Short Studies in
Systematic Theology

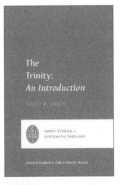
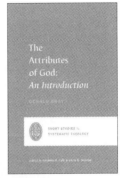

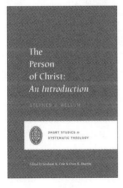
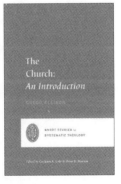

The Short Studies in Systematic Theology series aims to
equip readers to understand, teach, love, and apply what
God has revealed in Scripture about a variety of topics,
with each volume introducing a major systematic doctrine.

For more information, visit **crossway.org**.